PRAISE FOR "DOES GOD STILL BLESS THE U.S.A?"

Dear Lee,

Barbara and I are very happy that you have written a book issuing "A Plea for a Better America." Who better! You are an American icon, known and loved not only for the joy your music has brought to millions, but for your love of country and your unwavering support for our men and women in uniform.

You're a great American, Lee, and we Bushes treasure our friendship with you. We look forward to reading "Does God Still Bless the U.S.A.?" and wish you great success with the book.

—President, George H.W. Bush
Houston, Texas

"I've known Lee Greenwood for many years and worked with him on different occasions. He is a multi-talented entertainer whose contributions to country music are legendary. He has also offered support of our troops around the world and embraces this role. Not only has Lee written, "God Bless the U.S.A.," a song that moves us each and every time it is heard, he has now written a book that asks us to evaluate America's future. Congratulations, Lee! You are a true patriot and I wish you great success with the new book. Most of all, I hope those who read it are inspired to respect, protect and cherish our beloved nation as never before."

—Reba McEntire
Television Actress and Award-winning
Country Music Artist and Entertainer
Nashville, Tennessee

"Lee Greenwood's famous song "God Bless the U.S.A." is heard year round during the most special moments in the lives of Americans. Greenwood is not only an exceptional entertainer, but one who makes a difference and stands up for what he believes. I have personally been honored to work with him for many years for our Freedom Concert Series which have raised more than $10 million to benefit and provide scholarships for children of fallen heroes. Lee's new book "Does God Still Bless the U.S.A.?" delves deep into what matters most to Americans and what must be done to protect the sovereignty of this great nation. It is a must read for everyone who believes that God does in fact *still* bless the U.S.A."

—Sean Hannity
Radio and Television Host
Author of three New York Times best-selling Books
Political Commentator

"My friend, Lee Greenwood has served on the Board of Advisors with me and the Challenger families to honor the Space Shuttle Challenger crew and "Teacher in Space" mission. He is a true American patriot who represents all patriots, especially those who serve selflessly and courageously in our armed forces. He has blessed our nation with his many talents as a writer, entertainer and musician and created a national treasure in his song, "God Bless the U.S.A.". Considered by the military as *their* song, it is known the world over.

Lee is also a loving father and husband. Our family has been blessed by our friendship with the Greenwood family for many years and I know firsthand how Lee and Kim Greenwood exemplify the American spirit. Lee's new book, *Does God Still Bless the U.S.A.?* focuses on everything right about America and draws attention to some areas to guarantee her future greatness. The book is a must-read for all who love our country. You will be encouraged, challenged, and moved by its message, I promise."

—June Scobee Rodgers, Ph.D
Widow of Challenger Commander, Dick Scobee
Founding Chairman, Challenger Center

Almost thirty years ago, I became an instant Lee Greenwood fan the first time I heard *I.O.U.*, for which Lee won a Grammy Award in 1983. Shortly thereafter, I met Lee and discovered what a uniquely fascinating and multi-talented person he is. Then *God Bless the U.S.A.* was released, and overnight Lee evolved from country music star to beloved American icon. Lee has been a friend for more than a quarter-century, and during this time I have been so impressed with, but not at all surprised by, his indefatigable support for our country and for US troops serving around the world. There is no doubt Lee's song and his name will be equated with patriotism forever. I hope every citizen of our great country will read and be inspired by Lee's latest book, *Does God Still Bless the U.S.A.?*, and then share it with family and friends so that collectively we can endeavor to restore America's heart and soul. Congratulations, Lee…and thank you!

—Alex Gregory
Chairman, President & CEO
YKK Corporation of America
Atlanta, Georgia

"If you want to guarantee any event's success, just ask Lee Greenwood to show up and sing his signature song, God Bless the U. S. A.! Lee's willingness to perform at fund raising events here in Colorado for Volunteers of America has helped raise millions of dollars for this important organization we personally support. I, (Ernie) have also requested Lee to perform at Army vs. Navy and Navy vs. Air Force football games. The entire stadium of 80,000 sings along. Our friendship with the Greenwood family was forged through those events and we continue to enjoy our relationship with this warm, remarkable man and his family. I (Sharon) was recently honored to receive the Mizel Museum's Community Enrichment Award. Imagine how thrilled we were when Lee surprised us by coming to perform at the award ceremony. As he finished to thunderous applause, there was not a dry eye in the place.

Congratulations on 'Does God Bless the U.S.A.,' Lee. We believe you are the voice of thousands of dedicated citizens who cherish and proudly "stand up next to her." We hope the book's message reaches this generation and generations to come!"

—Ernie and Sharon Magness Blake
Philanthropists and Business Leaders
Ernie Blake, United States Naval Academy graduate, '64,
and former Mayor of Breckenridge, Colorado

"When most people think about Lee Greenwood it's the most natural thing in the world to start singing "God Bless The U.S.A." which in my opinion will be the most remembered and longest lasting patriotic song since the National Anthem.

But be that as it may, it is only one of the hits Lee has had. You don't sustain a successful and long lasting career like his without being an entertainer and Lee Greenwood is a superb entertainer and that's something either "you git it or you don't git it." Lee "gits" it.

Lee, my fellow entertainer, patriot, avid supporter of our military and *hale fellow well met*, may God bless you and our beloved U.S.A."

—Charlie Daniels
Country Artist and Award Winning Entertainer
Nashville, Tennessee

"God Bless the U.S.A." is more than a powerful and popular song. It is the passionate plea of a true patriot. It has been my joy to know Lee and Kim Greenwood since 2001. In August of that year, I became their pastor at First Baptist Church Sevierville, Tennessee. Less than two weeks later, September 11 shook our nation and when it did, Lee once again assumed the role of Ambassador of Encouragement to our country.

Lee is focused, driven by principle and priorities. He loves his Lord, his family, and his homeland. He can bring a room full of people to their feet or be at home at a church gym playing a pick-up game of basketball. He has written some of the most popular songs in recent history and yet Lee has also worked with children's choirs at his church. He has been a good friend and a great encourager to his pastor. "*Does*

God Still Bless the U.S.A.?" is a timely question in the uncertain times. If you desire to be challenged to go to the next level as a patriot and be encouraged as a citizen, this is a book that you need to read."

—Randy C. Davis,
Former Pastor of First Baptist Church,
Sevierville, Tennessee
Executive Director-Treasurer for
the Tennessee Baptist Convention
Nashville, Tennessee

"What do you call a guy who loves his country and our military so much that he would be willing to help support them at a moment's notice? I call him by his name…Lee Greenwood. Not only has Lee written a song that will go down in history as one of the most beloved anthems of patriotism, but he lives out his faith in God and country everyday. Gena and I are honored to call Lee and his wife, Kim, among our friends and congratulate Lee on this new book. "Does God Still Bless the U.S.A." raises some thought-provoking questions and asks us all to consider our part in maintaining our "sweet land of liberty" for future generations. This book's message will be felt long after the last page is read."

—Chuck Norris
Actor/ Author/ Martial Artist and Personal Fitness Advocate
Veteran of the United States Air Force

"I have to admit I'm one of those guys who is moved every single time I hear Lee Greenwood sing "God Bless the U.S.A." I think it moves me because I know Lee and I know his heart for our country and for our soldiers. I think it's more than just a song for me because it's more than just a song for Lee. And when I heard that he was writing a book about the issues that concern our homeland, I knew I had to read it. The book, just like the song, is a true reflection of his heart and a rallying point for all of us who love this country."

—Michael W. Smith, Singer/Songwriter
Nashville, Tennessee

Does
GOD
still bless
the USA?

LEE GREENWOOD

Does GOD *still bless* *the* USA?

A PLEA FOR A BETTER AMERICA

TATE PUBLISHING
AND ENTERPRISES, LLC

Published by Tate Publishing & Enterprises, LLC
127 E. Trade Center Terrace | Mustang, Oklahoma 73064 USA
1.888.361.9473 | www.tatepublishing.com

Tate Publishing is committed to excellence in the publishing industry. The company reflects the philosophy established by the founders, based on Psalm 68:11,
"The Lord gave the word and great was the company of those who published it."

Book design copyright © 2012 by Tate Publishing, LLC. All rights reserved.
Cover design by Leah LeFlore
Interior design by Nathan Harmony

Published in the United States of America

ISBN: 978-1-61777-444-7
1. Biography & Autobiography / Entertainment & Performing Arts
2. Religion / Religion, Politics & State
12.02.02

Table of Contents

13   Introduction by Lee Greenwood

★   (Lee receives hundreds of letters or emails every year from military personnel or their families thanking him for his song, "God Bless the U.S.A."—we have included only a few. They appear between the chapters, and are titled, Thanks for "God Bless the U.S.A.")

17   I'm Not Over 9/11

29   Whatever Happened to Integrity

45   The Battle for America's Soul

57   How's the Family?

77   Bashing America is "In"

89   Is America Still the Land of Opportunity?

105   Seriously, Does my Vote Count?

121   A Nation of Givers

135   Where are the Heroes?

157   DOES GOD STILL BLESS THE U.S.A.?

173   Special Thanks

175   30 DAY DEVOTIONAL "Prayers of a Patriot"

207   Photos

213   Other Information

Introduction

I was born at the beginning of the American dream. Depending on how you view the time line, I arrived at the onset of the baby-boom several years before Generation X. I was a child when patriotism was high and post-war optimism celebrated everything from the overall economy to a family's purchase of their first television set. It was a kinder world in many ways. You really knew your neighbors, kids congregated at the local burger joint, and you could get into a world of trouble for just sassing a teacher or getting caught with a cigarette.

Talk about change. In my lifetime I have seen our country surpass all others in economic development. We have gone to the moon and back and our technological advances boggle the mind. Some nerdy kids became multi-millionaires overnight with the invention of the internet. Through Facebook or YouTube, you can become famous overnight, as well. Seems like everyone is looking for their "fifteen minutes of fame." We can now go anywhere we choose, do anything we want, even be anyone you want. Plastic surgery can transform your face and body; can even change your sex. We have cell phones, ATM cards, cameras flying around in space, digital television, email, computers that run our lives at home and the office. Yet, amid all these wonderful achievements and potential, there is another side to our country that concerns me. Something is wrong and for the last few decades it seems that our beloved America is in danger of losing its heart; its soul.

Sure, the world calls us a super-power and we seem to be economically sound, even wealthy in comparison to other nations. Is this a façade? Debt has crippled families and foreclosures are at an all-time high. The national debt has now reached a staggering $15 trillion dollars. What does that fiscal bondage mean for my children and yours? Seems the more money we make, the more we want, and the less we actually have. As the financial crisis grows, is the country experiencing a spiritual or moral decline even more serious?

Our great urban cities are deteriorating. Drugs cross our borders and pour into our country with relative ease. Gang wars and related shootings are commonplace. With the increasing number of violent crimes, America now owns the highest incarceration rate in the world. There is also crisis in the education arena, unemployment, political posturing—did the boomer generation see it all coming or did we simply look away?

I wrote "God Bless the U.S.A." in 1983 and will be forever grateful for the song's impact. The song continues to be sung from coast to coast at events as grand as presidential command performances to simple county fairs. It is performed at rodeos, high school assemblies, on the Senate floor, at national memorial events, during soldiers' homecomings, at funerals, Super Bowls, and on and on; its legacy continues. I am busier than I have ever been and the song, of course, is the highlight of every show; the pivotal moment of every performance. Lately, as I come to the close of the song, "There ain't no doubt I love this land, God Bless the U.S.A." I invoke a simple, silent prayer, "God, we need you; please continue to bless us."

So, why this book; why now? Because I consider myself a patriot. The definition for a patriot is as follows: "One who loves and loyally, or zealously supports and defends one's own country." As a husband and father, I would confront anyone or anything who threatened the safety of my family. As Americans, it is time to confront the multiple risks that are threatening the prosperity and security of our nation.

You will hear a little about my life, my music, and my passions in this book. But for me there is no greater passion than to inspire others to do something to "right" our once proud ship of state, our beloved America. It is easy to become immune to the challenges and to view the battle as impossible to win. We need leadership, we need hope, and we need a renewed commitment to the real meaning of America. Most of all we need inspiration. Hopefully, you will find some in the following pages of "Does God Still Bless the U.S.A.?"

—Lee Greenwood

I'm Not Over 9/11

Thousands of lives were suddenly ended by evil, despicable acts of terror. The pictures of airplanes flying into buildings, fires burning, huge structures collapsing, have filled us with disbelief, terrible sadness and a quiet, unyielding anger.

—George W. Bush, president of the United States

All of a sudden there were people screaming. I saw people jumping out of the building. Their arms were flailing. I stopped taking pictures and started crying.

—Michael Walters, freelance photojournalist,
Manhattan

My wife and I made our way through the jutting shards of steel and buckled concrete—the remnants of the World Trade Center in New York City. Our emotions were raw and the unforgettable sights will linger for a lifetime. Like the rest of the nation, we had watched television images of the attack and aftermath, but no photos or television coverage had fully captured the devastation.

Only ten days after the attack, work was underway and we could hear engine noise from huge cranes removing mounds of debris. Gold bars buried under tons of dirt had not been excavated from the bank that had once been located on the site, so armed security personnel stood guard. The day we visited the site was the first day the operation turned from one of rescue to recovery; they no longer expected to find anyone alive. Yet there was still an inkling of hope. We heard the drills and pick axes hacking through granite and stone, searching for the remains of someone's spouse, parent, or child. Amid the noise, there was an eerie reverence, a sacred underlying stillness. Kim and I walked carefully among the broken slabs and choking dust, speaking to each other in hushed tones.

We had also visited the ferry, which was moored at the dock, where all the rescue workers went to grab a bite of lunch or take a quick break. The New Jersey police had brought us to the site by boat, along with a USO representative. As our group separated, each taking a different level of the boat, we spoke to as many workers as we could. Here we met some of the men and women from around the country who had come to New York City to offer their services. Exhausted from days of little or no sleep, they had been taking naps on cots set up in nearby gymnasiums. These selfless volunteers seemed stunned to hear that the prayers of a grateful nation were with them and that millions appreciated their efforts.

Leaving the ferry, we were escorted through gutted buildings closer to Ground Zero. Suddenly, I just felt it was the right thing to do. Stepping up onto jagged pieces of stone and metal, I didn't fight the emotion. I began to sing:

> And I'm proud to be an American
> where at least I know I'm free
> And I won't forget the men
> who died who gave that right to me …

One by one, others joined in and began singing with me as tough, gravelly-voiced men sang from their hearts. Kim later said, "A song I have heard hundreds of times suddenly had new meaning."

While walking Times Square on that first visit, we noticed how the usual hustle and bustle was missing. The ghostly silence of the Square was more deafening than the sounds of New York streets. During our stay at the Times Square Marriott Hotel, we shared an elevator ride with a woman carrying a stack of trays. Each tray contained numerous pieces of paper. Our curiosity was piqued and we asked the woman about them. She informed us that there was an on-site forensics lab in the hotel, where a team of technicians, were trying to identify body parts found at the World Trade Center site. We stood in disbelief, for no response seemed appropriate.

I've got to be honest… I am not over that feeling, that moment, that hurt, that wounded pride, that anger, that deep resolve. I'm not over 9/11.

—Lee

The weather is turning cooler here in Tennessee. Sitting on my back porch, I notice how almost overnight the leaves on our trees have changed to shades of yellow and orange and red. As I prepare to write this book, I realize that I've changed, too. The seasons of my life have taught me valuable lessons I couldn't have learned had I not been willing to change. Older and hopefully wiser, maturity has shifted some of my priorities through the years, but one commitment remains steadfast and intact. I still believe in the United States of America and what she stands for.

It has now been 11 years since that morning of September 11, 2001, when our innocence as a nation was shattered and Americans were shell-shocked following the destruction of the World Trade Center in New York City and the attack on the Pentagon.

Each 9/11 brings it all back. Like so many others, I remember where I was and how I reacted when I first heard the news.…

I was asleep in a hotel room in Los Angeles. A meeting had been scheduled with Gail Holcomb, an agent at the William Morris Agency, for later that morning. My wife's call woke me a little before 6 A.M.; 9 A.M. in the Smoky Mountains of Tennessee.

"Lee," Kim said excitedly, "turn on the television! Something terrible is happening!"

At that time the first tower had already been hit. Then I watched the coverage as the second hijacked plane blasted its way into the south tower. Both buildings would crumble before our eyes.

I heard the fear in Kim's voice, and it broke my heart. The terror she felt was shared by all; for the first time in US history, we had been attacked on our own native soil and this time by an enemy without a country. She also feared that Los Angeles would be targeted in some way. All domestic flights around the country were grounded in response to the events so I could not fly home to be with her and our boys, who were six and three years old at the time. In fact, I would not be able to make it back to Tennessee for another three weeks.

The next few hours were surreal. In the hotel lobby, people crowded around television monitors. Some shook their heads in disbelief, some wept openly, others looked dazed, confused. Out on the streets, people appeared to be in shock. A palpable sadness hovered over the scene. We were all anxious for further information about the tragedy. Every conversation included the questions, "Who would do this?" and "Why?"

Of course, in the next few days we would discover that the attacks on the World Trade Center and Pentagon were acts of terrorism directed to strike at the heart of America's financial institutions and our national symbol of military strength. It was several hours before we got the news of a fourth plane that went down in Pennsylvania and the brave Americans who sacrificed themselves to save another strike on innocent civilians. I truly believe that plane was headed for the White House.

The words "Let's roll" echo like the cannon at Ft. McHenry when another generation of Americans stood firm and sacrificed themselves to save our nation. Like everyone else, I became angry and wanted someone to be held accountable, some way to "get even." We were just beginning to understand the repercussions of the first acts of terrorism perpetrated on American soil.

Only a few days later I sat on a platform in Yankee Stadium with New York City dignitaries, including then Mayor Giuliani and President Clinton. The event was a memorial service dedicated to the fallen heroes of 9/11—the firemen and policemen who had lost their lives that day. Other performers, including Bette Midler and Marc Anthony, were on the program. Bette sang her trademark "Wind Beneath my Wings" and there was deep anguish, a heaviness in the stadium. A nation was in pain. I leaned in to Kim who sat beside me and whispered, "I feel inadequate and I'm not sure that 'God Bless the U.S.A.' is the right song for the moment. This is a time of mourning and reverence. I should be singing 'Amazing Grace.'"

Seconds later I was introduced. I was shaking as I walked to the stage with my head down. I began to sing my song:

If tomorrow all the things are gone I've worked for all my life...

While I sang the words, my thoughts shot back to my Grandmother Edna Jackson, who once said to me, "Lee, if you want to be remembered for something, make sure it is for something positive and good." *Grandma, is this what you meant?* I had sung my song, "God Bless the U.S.A.," countless times. This time I prayed it would be used more than ever before to encourage hurting hearts, that it would be "something positive and good," as Grandma had said.

I started the chorus:

I'm proud to be an American,
where at least I know I'm free.
And I won't forget the men
who died who gave that right to me.

Like a giant wave, the crowd began to stand. You could feel the shift of emotion as people held up photos of their loved ones—sons, husbands, mothers, daughters, parents and friends. They all sang with me, taking the event from a mood of mourning to a celebration of life. The song became the perfect avenue for thousands to express their appreciation for sacrifice and their pride in our great nation.

As I finished the song, I literally fell apart in tears. Marc Anthony embraced me as I walked from the stage. We stood there, two grown men, two grateful Americans weeping together on the field, giving each other strength. Kim later expressed, "I am so proud of you, Lee. God has used you to help heal and give voice to the pride of our nation."

I would sing "God Bless the U.S.A" again at Carnegie Hall for the policemen's memorial and then at the fourth game of the World Series in October of that same year. For three years following, Kim and I attended a Christmas event planned for family members of victims of 9/11. It was held on a stage set up on the street outside the New York Stock Exchange just blocks from the World Trade Center site. Mayor Rudy Giuliani was present, along with various athletes from New York teams, actors, politicians, singers and entertainers. We remember, especially that first year, seeing military snipers on the rooftops overlooking the stage. Many policemen and firemen attended the special program and expressed their gratitude for our coming.

Along with singing, I was asked to read "'Twas the Night Before Christmas.'" As I was introduced to read the book, a large group of children gathered in front of me. Their ages varied from infants, held on their mother's laps, to teens. Midway into the classic poem, I had a sobering realization: Each of those children had lost either a mother or a father on 9/11. Many in the audience and onstage were openly weeping as the program concluded. My eyes are full of tears as I write these words, remembering the tremendous emotion of that night.

Afterwards, Kim and I were privileged to visit personally with the hurting families. We listened to stories about fathers, brothers, husbands, sons, wives, and daughters who were lost only three short months before. We shared their pain, offered prayers and hugs, tried to speak words of encouragement and appreciation, but mainly…we just wept with them. Of course, we were thinking of our two young sons safe at home, while we embraced parents who had lost their precious children to this unfathomable tragedy.

Over the years, the event, though still difficult, has become more of a celebration of the brave men and women who had died. There was less emotion, fewer tears, but those in attendance remain grateful that we cared enough to remember their loved ones. We will never forget the day the skyline of New York City changed, but it's evident that New York and America is healing.

In the days following September 11, 2001, President Bush ordered troops into Afghanistan and Iraq. One specific question began to dominate my thoughts, a question I was asking for the first time, *Why do they hate us so?*

Who are these people and where are they from? Do they perceive we are somehow standing in their way? Are we keeping them from some eternal destiny they feel is theirs alone? What have we done that is so reprehensible as to make us the target of such deep, murderous hatred?

So, here we are, years later. Now we know that we will never be the same. There is a psychological term called "anticipatory anxiety," and we all had it immediately following September 11. The term refers to the reaction when you can't recover from one event for worrying about what is coming next. Many Americans remained afraid and anxious because we didn't know if there would be other attacks or where they would take place.

Remember the line in Joni Mitchell's song, "Big Yellow Taxi"? It says, "You don't know what you've got, 'til it's gone." After 9/11, we knew what was gone; we realized we were not invincible. Terrorism had come to us and accomplished, for a time, its goal—to instill fear and intimidation. The need to feel safe is so basic that we were asking, "Can we ever live normal lives again?"

National security was overhauled in every conceivable way. Armed air marshals boarded flights; check-in procedures and stringent identification measures were put in place at airports. You may recall how the government even beefed up security to our water supplies, oil storage tanks, and pipe line systems. New manuals were written on protecting government buildings. But a new reality settled in: All this would never be enough. No amount of caution, care, or preparedness could guarantee our safety.

There are not enough firemen, National Guard members, or policemen to guard every bridge, tunnel, commercial airport, bus or train station, highway, dam, or nuclear plant. It would be impossible. Not to mention trying to secure the millions of pieces of mail handled daily by the postal system. Again, impossible. Besides commercial flights, there are around 280,000 private planes that fly out of hundreds of small, unguarded airports. In fact, there are more flights per day in America than some countries log in a year. Imagine trying to track all of them. Sounds pretty hopeless doesn't it?

But here's the thing. The indomitable American spirit will not let terrorism win. We pulled together in the days that followed 9/11 and gained a new resolve. We were determined not to let the hijackers, al-Qaeda, Osama bin Laden, or any group on earth get away with it.

We found new heroes in the first responders on the scene at the World Trade Center. We hailed the bravery of those folks on board United Flight #93 who attacked the hijackers aboard their flight and saved many other lives by sacrificing their own. Patriotism was at an all-time high. Flag sales skyrocketed; you saw a flag on every car, house, crane, and bridge. My song, "God Bless the U.S.A." was also #1 on every chart in America. In record numbers our young men and women volunteered to serve in the military to protect our freedom. We took the opportunity to say thank you once more to our grandparents and great-grandparents who fought in World War II, Korea, and Vietnam. Across the country, in huge arenas or on tiny baseball fields where Little League games were played, we once again wept when the strains of the beloved "Star Spangled Banner" were played.

Remember? It was as if we woke up, realized how precious our freedom is, and became determined again to hold on to it, fight for it, even die for it. We stood behind our president and his decisions to pursue the perpetrators of 9/11. We had a common enemy and the labels "Republican" or "Democrat" fell by the wayside as we united to confront and battle terrorism.

Then, as the war in Iran and Afghanistan began to claim more and more lives, it became clear it was not going to be an "easy in–easy out" situation. The war, heralded at first, soon sparked controversy. No weapons of mass destruction were found in Saddam Hussein's Iraq and the Democrats cried, "Foul! We entered the war under false pretenses." At that juncture, President Bush and his advisors were considered the culprits, not the saviors. The country was soon divided between those who wanted American troops withdrawn and sent home and those who believed we were fighting terrorists over there to keep them from coming over here. Some felt we were involved in a lot of things worldwide that were "none of our business" and we needed to overhaul our foreign policy completely. Even the new administration of 2008 realized that their campaign promises to end the war in two years were extremely premature and unrealistic. To date, Operation Iraqi Freedom and Enduring Freedom in Afghanistan have claimed nearly 6,000 American lives. Debate continues and the disagreement remains as to how to end the war with our honor intact and our country safe.

But the ongoing war is not the only divisive issue in America. We are poles apart on several issues that our parents and especially our grandparents would never have thought it necessary to discuss. Yet there was a time when America was known as a Christian, God-fearing nation. Can that be said of her still, when religion has been all but banned from public expression of any kind? The divide between a religious-based society and a secular society gets wider and wider.

The extent of government participation in our lives is another hot-button topic. Some Americans feel it is perfectly okay for government to "bail out" financial institutions who used poor, even criminal business principles, but do not want the government to meddle in our private lives or set moral boundaries of any kind. Congress is almost evenly split between Republicans and Democrats. Without someone coming to the middle, it will continue to be deeply divided and dysfunctional.

It is safe to say, we have never been more divided as a nation. Besides the internal pressures, there is the remaining threat of more terrorism attacks. We are hated by other nations for what we have, for our leadership, for our influence, so I believe there may be other attempts to cripple our defenses, stifle our economy, and erode our core beliefs.

In the midst of all this upheaval, are we teaching our children what patriotism means? Where are the role models? There has never been a greater need for a return to true patriotism.

Many still ask what inspired me to write "God Bless the U.S.A." The song was a response to the hurt and anger I felt after the downing of a Korean jet on a flight from New York to Seoul in 1983, with 269 passengers aboard, including 63 Americans. Russian authorities shot the plane from the sky, killing all aboard because "they thought the airliner was on a spy mission." Civilians? On a spy mission? Unbelievable! Soviet officials reported that the plane was flying without navigation lights and that the crew refused to acknowledge signals from pursuing Soviet fighters. I could not forget the scenes of weeping men, women, and children who had just been told the grim news that their loved ones would never return. I saw the senseless strike as a personal attack against our countrymen and it moved me to put pen to paper. The song came so easily, it nearly wrote itself.

I also drew upon my experiences as a boy being raised on my grandparents' farm and how my grandfather and grandmother had worked hard all of their lives to own and operate their farm. I remembered, too, when times got tough and how they lost their land, their livelihood…

If tomorrow all the things are gone I've worked for all my life
And I had to start again with just my children and my wife.
I'd thank my lucky stars to be livin' here today,
Where the flag still stands for freedom and they can't take that away.

Did I know the song was special, a hit from the beginning? Well, every time you go into the studio to record a song, you think it is going to be a hit. But, yes, I knew this song was special because of the response we received whenever we sang it live. We began to make it our closer for every performance and the audience responded emotionally, enthusiastically each time. I have been gratified to find out how much "God Bless the U.S.A." means to people, especially our military personnel and veterans.

Music has power within itself, but when the right words, melody, and emotion come together in one song, it is a beautiful thing. The song has now found its place in history, but my hope is that it endures and continues to be meaningful to people for generations to come. Like the song, this book is also a personal response to a crisis: our country's need for unity, integrity, healing, and faith.

In the following pages you will learn what I believe, you will hear my heart and hopefully share my vision for the future. You will understand why I felt an urgency to say some things I was feeling before it was too late. It was important to me that day in 1983 when I wrote "God Bless the U.S.A." and it is important to me today. I don't know about you, but I have not gotten over 9/11... I hope I never do.

Thanks for "God Bless the U.S. A."

Mr. Greenwood,

Thank you for allowing us to play "God Bless the U.S.A." at our son's funeral. We had it played as they were bringing Pat into the church at the beginning of the service.

Pat was one of the souls lost on August 6th in Afghanistan. He loved your song, and fit the profile to a tee. Pat told me that he wanted "God Bless the U.S.A." played at his funeral if he didn't make it back.

Pat was proud to be an American and serve his country. Pat died doing what he felt was his duty. That doesn't ease our pain much, but we hope in time it will.

Thank you, Mr. Greenwood

—DeLayne and Joyce Peck,
Parents of SSG Patrick D. Hamburger, killed
in action on August 6, 2011 in Afghanistan

Whatever Happened To Integrity?

No one will question your integrity if your integrity is not questionable.

—Nathaniel Bronner, Jr.

Integrity is doing the right thing, even if nobody is watching.

—Unknown

Through the glare of 24-hour cable news cycles, we have seen sports figures, religious and political heroes fall from grace with a resounding thud. We have watched our nation's major financial institutions crumble under the weight of greed. We have sympathized with the anguish of reported thousands who lost their life savings due to the selfish corruption of men who were more concerned with maintaining lavish lifestyles than being honorable. Lack of integrity seems to be at an all-time high in America...or is it?

When reading the Bible, I have been struck with how human nature hasn't changed much over thousands of years. Even "a man after God's own heart," King David in the Old Testament, gave in to lust and committed murder to claim another man's wife. Just imagine how David would have fared under the scrutiny of our present-day media. Men (and women) today succumb to the same vices: power, sex, hunger for control and greed. I argue that human nature has not changed, but because we live in this "information age," we hear more about the failures of public figures than ever before. When one steps outside the will of God, he or she loses focus of the ultimate purpose and sacrifices personal integrity.

Most of what I know about integrity I learned from my grandparents on the farm. I grew up in a city where two rivers converge; in fact, Sacramento, California is often referred to as "River City." The Sacramento of the '50s and '60s still had a small-town feel because it consisted of several small communities that eventually just grew together. The state capital was historic, with a Spanish influence like many California towns. I lived in North Sacramento, where rural farmlands stretched for miles around.

For as far back as I can remember, I worked alongside my grandfather, helping him tend to all the chores on the farm. Whether it was feeding the chickens, driving the tractor, or digging ditches, hard work was part of learning to be a man. Back in those days, a handshake sealed the deal and your word was as good as the gold discovered at nearby Sutter's Fort. Along with my grandfather, the women who raised me—my mother and grandmother—also made sure I understood that women were to be respected, revered, and protected.

When my musical gifts began to emerge, I carried those same values into performing—playing and singing locally and learning how to make a living by doing what I loved. A strong work ethic was part of my inbred culture. So was integrity. I knew that a man's word was important in measuring and defining a person's character.

Attending the First Baptist Church in North Sacramento further helped to solidify the value of making the "right" choices in life. As a kid at Hagginwood Elementary, Los Palmas Junior High, and later at Norte Del Rio High School, I never dreamed that one day I would be amazed at the widespread lack of integrity in almost every area of American business and government.

So how did we get here? Along with a struggling economy, unemployment on the rise, broken campaign promises, false advertising, and a media obsessed with sensationalism, integrity has taken a huge hit. In fact, it has reached an all-time low. Has compromise become a way of life? Are we losing the best of ourselves due to the lack of moral vision and integrity? Perhaps we need a revolution of sorts. A statement attributed to George Orwell says, "In a time of universal deceit, telling the truth is a revolutionary act."

And here's the truth as I see it. America must return to foundational tenets of faith that led men to live with integrity. There is a verse in the Bible that says it perfectly.

> Who may dwell with God on His holy hill? He who walks with integrity, works righteousness and speaks the truth in his heart.
>
> Psalm 15:1, 2

—Lee

★   ★   ★

Have all the citizens of this country lost their moral compass? Across the board in every profession, evidence of improprieties, sexual misconduct, theft, fraud, and misrepresentation is being reported. If that were not bad enough, the perpetrators include teachers, pastors, business leaders, government officials, sports figures, and others who ought to know better. With ethical or moral failures abounding from the White House down, Americans have nearly been desensitized when hearing about yet another cover-up or scheme to deceive.

Do our children perceive that everyone fails morally at some point and that it's somehow okay? Do they hear about unethical behavior so often that they believe such behavior should be expected because we are "human" and "no one is perfect"?

Here are some disturbing facts from the American Ethics Commission: 75 percent of the people applying for employment lie about something on their resume; 80 percent of high school students say they have cheated and will continue to cheat in order to make expected grades. More than half of all students surveyed said they didn't think cheating was a big deal; 40 percent of Americans do not report accurate income or tax information; although 90 percent of Americans believe adultery is wrong, 40 to 60 percent of all married couples will have at least one affair during their marriage. A whopping 70 percent believe that lying is okay (even necessary at times) as long as the lie doesn't hurt someone else.

With figures that confirm we are experiencing unprecedented moral challenges in our country, how do we teach our children that America is better than this? How do we train them to make integrity-driven choices? When I speak to my sons about the moral slips people make, we discuss the subject of integrity, not as generally defined, but in its broadest application. My definition of an integrity-driven person is simple—one who is true to his or her word and tells the truth. The integrity-driven person will do the right thing, not the easiest thing.

The word *integrity* comes from a Latin phrase that means "wholeness" or "oneness." Those who suffer from a lack of integrity, like the examples mentioned above, are simply not "whole." I, myself, have learned that lesson more than once.

So who is the person you would trust with your life? A friend, a family member? Is there someone in whom you have complete confidence? There really is no greater compliment than to be the one whom others trust. This person is consistent, truthful, dependable. You would give him access to your bank account and never worry about missing a penny. Why? Because he has integrity.

Readers probably assume that there is less integrity in my business, the entertainment business, than in any other profession. I don't believe that has ever been true. Today, moral compromise is widespread and found in every facet of American life. Sure, there is greed, unscrupulous agents, scheming PR people in the music business, but there are also some very decent, moral, "salt-of-the-earth" men and women who live clean, wholesome lives everyday.

I was a young teenager, fourteen years of age, when I started in this business. I learned quickly to spot those people who wanted to use me for their own financial or personal gain. But I didn't always see it coming. Once, a former manager convinced our young band to purchase a nightclub in Idaho Falls, Idaho. We had to perform there several weeks for free just to make ends meet. It was a losing proposition from the start, but we tried to make it go. Then the manager who talked us into the deal took off with the profits the club made that year, leaving us with nothing but the huge debt. He stole it all. After that, I paid more attention to judging the character of those with whom I worked.

Of course, there were other occasions when I was disappointed with people I trusted. One of the unwritten rules of the road for musicians is that you don't quit a band without a replacement being hired in your place. On another occasion, when we were in Alaska on tour, a guy in our band gave me notice that he would be leaving us in two days to join another group. Two days? Did I mention we were in *Alaska?* The situation for us was impossible, but he obviously didn't care. He saw the move as a step up, so he stepped on others and sacrificed all integrity to get ahead. That was a hard one to put behind me.

Over the years, I have become adamant about making sure the people who work for us know there are some behaviors so detrimental to the group they are grounds for dismissal. Drugs, drunkenness, or abusive behavior of any kind will simply not be tolerated. My reputation is at stake. Lying is a serious infraction to me. I can forgive a lie the first time, but repeated lying and deception are not acceptable. Other entertainers may be looser with rules and standards but, for me, parameters and boundaries must be established for everyone's benefit. It is a part of being integrity-driven.

While I am extremely proud of the work ethic I have tried to bring to my profession, I have certainly made my share of mistakes in my own personal life. After all, I was a part of the '60s generation and while I had no interest in alcohol or drugs, the "feel good" generation did affect me. The music business mantra was: "Sex, drugs, and rock 'n roll." I just left out the "drugs" part. I look back on those years with much regret. I wasted so much time and energy. However, now I believe I have regained personal integrity by realizing what is really important. I have placed a greater value on my marriage, being a father and a man of God.

I have made some dumb choices in my life and have had to face some pretty stiff consequences. The wonderful thing about maturity is that eventually you should learn from your mistakes. I can honestly say that God has used each and every experience in my life, good and bad, to chisel me into the man He always knew I could become. I'm still a work in progress. I pray my family sees my dedication to them and that I have laid the groundwork for their security and safety. I hope they can say I am a good husband and a good father. I want to be a man of integrity in their eyes.

Band of Brothers

I have been blessed and inspired through powerful friendships with some extraordinary men. First, I have to mention my manager of thirty years, Jerry Bentley. He is a former Marine who was wounded while serving in Viet Nam. He is a man of discipline, integrity, strength, and has a powerful work ethic. He has stood by me through thick and thin and is respected by all who know him. He is more than a manager, he is my friend. Jerry's wife, Elaine, has been extremely understanding about the many hours, days and weeks he has given to my career. It's enormously helpful to have someone like Jerry who does a great job representing me, but is also well respected in the industry.

Secondly, I need to mention Alex Gregory. We met about twenty-seven years ago while I was touring in Georgia. He is currently the President, Chairman, and CEO of the YKK Corporation. His title does not reflect his heart. His genuine understanding for people and their daily trials has taught me much. He is fluent in Japanese and due to his international travel, Alex has a worldly view of events and how they affect people in his company and his own family. He is a great example of humility and has shared with me the importance of being genuinely happy. He gave me the Bible I carry and use every day in my prayer time. When I need someone to talk to for advice, Alex is my second call, right after my wife.

I hesitate to mention all my friends by name, but my life was forever changed also, when I met two self-described "Florida crackers"—my great friends, Walt McLin and Dewey Burnsed, both attorneys and real gentlemen. Walt and Dewey entered my life as investors in my career before anyone knew who I was. Throughout our friendship of many years, I learned from them the importance of "working to live" and not "living to work." Walt would question me about my direction in life, seeing through my attempts to be guarded and secretive. Walt was a man above reproach and he set a standard for me I admired and leaned upon. I learned the value of hearty laughter during evenings at their poker table. Through them, I learned to have a zest for living each day to the fullest and the importance of having someone who holds you accountable. I am a better man because of my friendship with Walt and Dewey and am still heartbroken over losing them a few years ago when they passed away only two weeks apart. But my relationship with the McLin and Burnsed families remains strong, and I hope my children will continue to be friends with them all their lives.

Today, I enjoy the fellowship of several guys I call my "accountability group"—men in positions of authority, including two pastors, whom I often speak with before a public performance. I know the "accountability" concept isn't new to most people, but I'm grateful for these men who help me "keep it real." We hold each other to a very high standard and pray for each other and our families. Life is hard and Satan is crafty. His most common trick is to make really stupid decisions seem like the right thing to do—the ultimate goal being our death and destruction (see 1 Peter 5:8).

One of my favorite quotes says, "It's hard to fly like an eagle when you're surrounded by turkeys." I must admit, there were times in my past when I was part of the "turkey" crowd, and I regret those days.

God was smiling on me when He sent me my wife, Kim. (See Chapter 4 about how we met). When I fell in love with Kim, I fell in love for the first time. I was struck by her beauty, but also captured by her passion for life. We've been married nearly twenty years at the time of this writing, and Kim makes me feel like a king in our home. She is a former Miss Tennessee USA, who will always be my queen. We have traveled the world together, and I can count on Kim's unfailing support with every new endeavor or dream. Kim is the love of my life and my spiritual beacon. "Thank You, God, for sending me an angel."

I loved my grandparents, Edna and Thomas Jackson, but faith was not evident in our home as I was growing up. I was shown the value of integrity and hard work, but there was no prayer. My grandparents *sent* me to church, but never *took* me to church. I didn't know my father until I was a teenager, and my mother was in and out of several marriages, which didn't add to my stability as a youngster. So, when I married Kim, I inherited a wonderful family as well—the Payne family. Kim's parents, Jim and Pauline; her grandparents, Lindsey and Jennie Ann; Kim's brother Andy—a family focused on following God's will in all things. Their family values epitomize integrity and I remain honored that they have accepted me wholeheartedly.

I am also proud to say that two men I admire most are my sons, Dalton and Parker. Though still young, the earmarks of great courage, strength, intellect, and integrity are evident in their lives. This country I love is a better place because they are citizens.

The Big Picture

For most of my life, I focused on my career and taking my talent as far as it would go. I rarely took the time to examine the "big picture." I never asked myself *why* God gave me this talent to write and sing. Now I often ask, "God, how can I best use my talent for Your glory?" I now realize with great power, talent, or success comes great responsibility. I am both honored and humbled to see how God has used my life—yes, even my mistake-filled life—for a greater good. That's the amazing thing about God—His grace ultimately redeems us of our sin, accepts us with all our flaws and uses us, even with all our bumps and bruises, to inspire and strengthen others.

While God hasn't used my life in the same way, I identify with David, the shepherd boy who became Israel's king. He was a songwriter, also; we are both fallen men whom God still chose to inspire others. David's songs of praise to God have prevailed through generations. My prayer is that "God bless the U.S.A." will endure also as a song of thanks to God for our beloved country—the nation "under God" which Ronald Reagan referred to as the "shining city upon a hill." Time will tell.

Integrity Starts in the Home

The "Golden Rule" is still the best measure to use when teaching our children to live with integrity. "Do unto others as you would have them do unto you" still works in any situation. This basic truth must be instilled into our children. It's a good rule to live by, and parents must be the ones to model this principle for their children.

More than ever, sports enthusiasts, coaches, and educators are concerned about the behavior and attitude of parents involved in their child's activities. There have always been reports of arguments and shouting matches between over-competitive mothers and fathers regarding their children's athletic endeavors, but now competitiveness has taken a new and dangerous turn. There are accounts across the country of parents who have physically attacked their son's or daughter's coaches, teachers, or someone else in the stands. This should alarm all of us.

The most publicized was the case of Thomas Junta, a Boston father charged with killing his son's ice hockey coach after a fight broke out between the two at the end of practice. In full view of children, ages ten to fifteen, Junta repeatedly pounded the coach's head on the rink floor, severing arteries and sending the coach to the hospital in a coma. He died two days later. Are you ready for this? Junta's complaint was he felt the coach was allowing too much physical contact between the children. His sentence was six to ten years for involuntary manslaughter. Other parents in the stands testified how Junta was constantly attempting to make other parents his allies in the stands when complaining about the coaching. What a great example to kids, right?

We need to get back to the practice of requiring our children to show respect for those in authority, such as teachers, coaches, policemen, and especially their own parents. This is an important part of teaching a child to live with integrity. Parents who disregard authority, use profanity, and are angry and belligerent people are raising children who repeat their behavior and end up crowding our already overloaded prison systems.

Integrity under Pressure

I see integrity as a fight for right—good versus evil. This is a battle we fight everyday. My grandfather often said, "The road to hell is paved with good intentions." You can have great intentions and want to do what is right, but the problem is, while we may know our intentions, others do not. The public will look only at our behavior and performance and will judge us accordingly. Our children must understand that lying, cheating, stealing, and disregarding the rights of others may start small but will set a pattern for life if left unchecked. It's the small things that grow into big things.

In early May of 2010, Nashville and all of middle Tennessee experienced torrential rains that left the area devastated by flooding. Damage in Nashville alone reached over one billion dollars. Nearly every aspect of the music industry and every part of town was impacted in some way by the floods. The record-breaking flood waters put pressure on every dam site in the area. The Percy Priest Dam isn't far from our home. If it had failed, downtown Nashville would have been lost and the damage would have been even worse than it was. Sadly, thirty-one people lost their lives in Tennessee, Kentucky, and Mississippi due to the floods. Experiencing those dark days, I remember being amazed at how the old dams took the pounding and relentless pressure. That is real strength.

Likewise, if we aspire to be integrity-driven, we, too, must be that strong.

Even in the face of unrelenting pressure, our value system must hold firm.

America's Return to Integrity

America needs a revival of integrity, starting at the top. I am well aware that some believe we should not hold our business or government leaders morally accountable. When a former president's indiscretions were brought to light, the debate centered around whether or not ethics should even be considered as long as he was doing a good job as president. Really? It should matter and matter big time! It's like a father who says, "Do as I say, not as I do." If the boss is dishonest, you can't expect employees to be honest. Those in leadership must realize they are being watched and will be held accountable for their actions.

On the political front, I am not advocating that we become a nation of witch-hunters or that we try to legislate morality, but we need to make it clear with our selection of candidates that integrity matters.

Same with business. Are we still offering Business Ethics 101? It will take years for the public's trust to be reestablished, if ever, in the face of government bailouts and business executives taking in millions of dollars in bonuses while cutting salaries and/or laying off thousands of regular workers. Half of all adults surveyed for a *Business Weekly* article felt that Wall Street was so focused on making money that it would break laws to do so, especially if it thought it could get away with it. No honor, no dignity, just basic greed at its worst.

Over the years I have witnessed the advantages of performing and managing a band with a reputation for having integrity. It really is no different than having to make ethical decisions personally on a daily basis. It may start with getting out of bed in the morning. Do I get up, or do I hit the snooze button and sleep in when I have responsibilities? Do I get to work in plenty of time, or am I late? Do I finish the tasks assigned to me, or am I undependable? Will I resist the temptation to take a few bucks out of the cash drawer? Will I pad my expense reimbursement request? Cheat on my taxes? These are choices we make individually every day.

When our children need a simple definition of unethical behavior, perhaps the clearest explanation is this: Unethical behavior is anything you would *not* want showing up on the front page of the newspaper. In that respect, values like honesty, openness, respect, and integrity should be continually emphasized as the most important assets of anyone's character.

What does integrity look like? It looks like Hayley Milbourne, a young woman golfer I read about recently. Hayley competed in the Interscholastic Athletic Association of Maryland's Golf Championship in 2007. She had won the event twice before. At the end of a round, she noticed she had actually been playing someone else's ball. No one else knew about the mistake. She legitimately had the winning score for the day, but she reported her mistake, although she knew it would keep her from winning the tournament. That is integrity.

Integrity looks like PeeWee Reese, who once played for the Brooklyn Dodgers. When Jackie Robinson took the field for the first time as the nation's first African-American to play major league baseball in 1947, fans shouted racial slurs and harassed Robinson, while some of the white players said they wouldn't take the field if Robinson played. Reese silenced the crowd when he walked over to Robinson, threw his arm around him in a friendly embrace that said, "I respect you. Welcome to the game." Robinson become one of the greatest players of baseball's modern era. Men and women of integrity reject bigotry and racism and are unswayed by crowd opinion. They stand for what is right.

Integrity looks like Eric Liddell, the "Flying Scotsman," subject of the award-winning movie, *Chariots of Fire*. In 1924, Liddell had trained and was the favorite to win the 100 meter race at the Paris Olympics. However, when the schedule was made public, Liddell announced he would not be running in the race because it was scheduled on a Sunday, and he felt "he would dishonor God by competing on the Lord's day." Fans were shocked and fellow competitors called him a fool, but Liddell stood firm. The Scotsman entered, instead, the 400 meter race, which he had never run and had never trained for. It became *his* race and history was made the day he won the gold. Sally Magnusen wrote in her book, *The Flying Scotsman*, that one reporter commented, "The lad is a true man of principle."

Many fine examples of integrity can also be found in the lives of American forefathers throughout our nation's history. The 19th century politician, Henry Clay, said, "I'd rather be right than be president." In 1809, Thomas Jefferson voiced what I believe should be every politician's mantra: "I never did, or countenanced, in public life, a single act inconsistent with the strictest good faith; having never believed there was one code of morality for a public, and another for a private man."

Can we build integrity into our children? I hope with all my heart that I am modeling integrity for my sons, but I'm not foolish enough to believe they won't make their own mistakes. I pray those mistakes are not of epic proportions. Mistakes often teach us some of life's most valuable lessons. Regardless the nature of our human struggles, most of life's trials are going to cause some discomfort, some pain. That very pain is life's greatest training ground. C.S. Lewis, in his classic, *The Problem of Pain,* said, "God whispers to us in our pleasures, speaks in our conscience, but shouts in our pains: it is His megaphone to rouse a deaf world." Ultimately, we can come through life's greatest challenges, listen and feel the pain they cause, and understand that God can use those experiences to draw us to Himself and discover our true purpose. It is in these times, God is yelling at us with His "megaphone."

Again, like morality, I don't believe integrity can be legislated. I do, however, believe that each American *can* determine to personally embrace its value. In January of 2011, United States Congresswoman from Arizona, Gabrielle Giffords, along with several others, were shot by a mentally unstable young man. My fifteen-year-old son Dalton was listening to the various pundits blame the heinous shooting on "inflammable political rhetoric." He turned to me and said, "Dad, do they really believe political discord led the man to open fire on inno-cent people? What about personal responsibility?" Even at fifteen, Dalton knows if he were to do something wrong, there would be no way he could blame someone else for his actions and get away with it—not in our household. Likewise, Americans need to stop blaming others, take personal responsibility for our own poor decisions, and dedicate ourselves anew to personal excellence and integrity.

As a Christian, I don't believe it is my role to judge others. Jesus came to earth not to condemn us, but to save us (see John 3:17). I gen-uinely hurt for those who find themselves victims of their own lack of integrity. One person's poor choice, moment of compromise, or moral weakness can cause a lifetime of hurtful consequences for others, too.

I strongly encourage Americans to pursue integrity in every aspect of their lives. I believe God will honor our efforts and continue to bless the U.S.A. when men and women of all races, faiths, and political persuasions determine to do so.

Thanks for "God Bless the U.S. A."

To Whom It May Concern:

I just wanted Lee Greenwood to know how much joy a stuffed bear dressed like a soldier that plays his song, "God Bless the U.S.A." brought to a badly wounded soldier at Brooke Army Medical Center at Ft. Sam Houston, Texas.

The bear was given to me because of my love for the song and for our military. I found out that one of "my kids" has been wounded in an IED explosion and was transported from Afghanistan to Brooke Medical Center. He has been in ICU for five weeks but has just been moved to a room. His name is Marcus Carr. I sent the bear to him because he was withdrawn and weak. He got it on Sunday and has held on to it and played Lee's song over and over. He shows it and plays it for everyone who comes into the hospital room.

One of my Daughters of American Revolution friends went to check on Marcus yesterday and he was sleeping while holding the bear under his arm. The point of this story is to let Lee know how his song has brought much happiness to this wounded soldier.

I am a strong supporter of our military and host homecoming parties at my home for returning military several times a year. It is my joy to do so.

—Dottie Wainwright
State Chairwoman and National Vice
Chairwoman– D A R Project Patriot
The Woodlands, Texas.

Battle for America's Soul

> The general principles on which our fathers achieved independence were the general principles of Christianity.
>
> —John Adams

> It cannot be emphasized too strongly or too often that this great nation was founded not by religionists, but by Christians: not on religions, but on the gospel of Jesus Christ.
>
> —Patrick Henry

> God who gave us life, gave us liberty.
>
> —Thomas Jefferson

> Blessed is the nation whose God is the Lord. The people He has chosen as His own inheritance.
>
> —Psalm 33:12

I am, without apology, a conservative. I am also a Christian. By putting those two words together—*Christian conservative*—I am aware that some will label me "politically incorrect" and disregard what I have to say in this chapter. However, the word *conservative* itself isn't so bad. It simply refers to one who "conserves," "keeps guard," or "closely observes." Among those things Americans should guard and treasure most is our Christian heritage. Many on both sides of the aisle, Republicans and Democrats, feel the same way.

If I were to name the single most destructive attack on our American way of life, it would be the push to eliminate any reference to God from our culture. There is one problem, however, with these attempts. You can't write God out of our history! His presence was relevant when the nation was founded, and it is still relevant for the majority of Americans today.

When prayer and Bible reading were banned from schools in the early '60s, it became apparent that there was a faction in our society intent on eradicating any public acknowledgment of God. One of the litigants in the lawsuit resulting in the ruling was atheist Madelyn Murray-O'Hair. It must have been the high point of her life to see such a landmark decision.

While Murray-O'Hair took full credit for the Court's decision on prayer, the ruling shocked the Christian community and put them on notice that this fight was only the first of many the atheists, who tout separation of church and state, would be determined to win. I find it compelling that the very court that deemed prayer unconstitutional begins everyday with this invocation: "God save the United States and this honorable court." It has been that way for the past two hundred years.

There is a battle for America's soul and we should take seriously the insidious threat to destroy our country's deep spiritual roots.

—Lee Greenwood

★　　★　　★

For most Americans, God is the cornerstone of our freedom and unique existence. We are a religious people. God is intrinsic to who we are, an undeniable part of our history. Yet, it seems there are some who are embarrassed or uncomfortable with our Christian heritage. I have traveled to many countries around the world and have never once been offended when I saw citizens of another country expressing worship to their deity of choice. I wasn't offended to hear someone praying in a mosque or Buddhist temple. I understood their worship as part of their culture. I didn't participate in the worship nor did I ever feel pressure to join that form of worship. But, I certainly didn't call my lawyer to see if we could sue just because I witnessed it. I share the feelings of Andy Rooney, the columnist who appeared for many years on the news program "60 Minutes." He wrote the following:

> I don't believe in Santa Claus, but I'm not going to sue somebody for singing a Ho-Ho-Ho song in December. I don't agree with Darwin, but I didn't go out and hire a lawyer when my high school teacher taught his theory of evolution. Life, liberty, or your pursuit of happiness will not be endangered because someone says a 30-second prayer before a football game. So what's the big deal? They're just talking to a God they believe in and asking Him to grant safety to the players on the field and the fans going home from the game.
>
> But it's a Christian prayer, some will argue. Yes, and this is the United States of America, a country founded on Christian principles. So what would you expect…somebody chanting Hare Krishna?
>
> If I went to a football game in Jerusalem, I would expect to hear a Jewish prayer. If I went to a soccer game in Baghdad, I would expect to hear a Muslim prayer. If I went to a ping pong match in China, I would expect to hear someone pray to Buddha. And I wouldn't be offended. It wouldn't bother me one bit. When in Rome.
>
> But what about the atheists? Well, no one is asking them to be baptized. We're not going to pass the collection plate. Just humor us for 30 seconds. If that's asking too much, bring a Walkman or a pair of ear plugs. Go to the bathroom. Visit the concession stand. Call your lawyer! Or just exercise your right to leave the country!

I couldn't agree more, Mr. Rooney. So, why is the secular left so opposed to religious expression being part of our cultural history? By the way, the word *secular* simply means "not overtly or specifically religious." Do they feel it too old-fashioned to believe in a Supreme Being? Is God or religion somehow threatening or frightening to them? I believe there are some who fear we will become too overt in our religious expression, too imbalanced and unfair to other religions if we don't keep a tight lid on expressions of Christian faith. So, in an effort to appease everyone, part of our rich, historical, and fundamental rights are being stripped away. We should keep reminding ourselves during this time that no law or political maneuver can strip what is firmly implanted in our hearts.

Prayer is very real to me. It releases my inner thoughts and turns them over to God, whom I believe is listening. I attended church early in my life mainly because I loved singing in the choir. Choir practices were on Wednesday nights and I never missed. I worked long hours alongside my grandfather and had little time to make friends. To their credit, my grandparents saw the importance of exposing me to spiritual things. I prayed when situations were dire, when I was desperate, when the need was intense.

It wasn't until later in my life, however, that prayer became a joyful ritual, a daily appointment with God, the outgrowth of a personal relationship with Christ. My wife, Kim, and I set aside time daily for personal devotions—a quiet time for prayer and meditation and even a time to listen to the Lord speak to us individually. Prayer is also an important part of our family life. There is no need, too big or too small, that we don't pause, along with our boys, to take it to the Lord in prayer.

Do I believe God still performs miracles? Absolutely! We may never even be aware of how many times God has intervened to protect, guide, or direct our lives. Miracles are happening everyday for those who believe and trust in the goodness and faithfulness of God. Our first son, Dalton, was diagnosed with a possible serious kidney condition when Kim went in for an unscheduled ultrasound before his birth. The danger of his losing a kidney became very real if the condition persisted. When Dalton was around three months old, Kim's grandfather, Lindsey Payne, respectfully asked if his pastor and the church leadership of First Baptist Church of Leesburg, Florida, could lay hands on Dalton and pray for complete healing. We eagerly agreed. Lindsey just could not bear the thought of Dalton undergoing such major surgery at such a young age. I remember how Kim and I continued to pray, and we asked others to pray for Dalton. Surgery was scheduled for a few weeks later.

On the morning of the surgery, doctors were explaining the procedure to Kim when she felt compelled to ask the pediatric urologist to perform one more test. She explained to him how many people had been praying for Dalton. The urologist smiled gently and agreed to another test while the baby was sedated for surgery. They wanted to check also to see if the other kidney had been affected in any way. We surrendered Dalton to the anesthesiologist, Houston White. His voice was reassuring as he promised to take care of Dalton like his own child. We made eye contact and I saw faith and trust in him. I will never forget sitting with Kim's parents and others in the hospital waiting room to hear the results of the doctor's examination. Thirty minutes later, we learned the outcome of the test. Much to our joy, nothing was wrong with either kidney! Imagine the jubilation when the doctor reported that there was no need for surgery—the situation had righted itself. Of course, we knew God had intervened in answer to our prayers. Dr. White was the anesthesiologist for the birth of both our sons. He was called home in 2011. I sang at his funeral.

Prayer is not just asking for things, it is praise, it is expressing thanks, and it is the acknowledgment of a personal relationship with a God who loves us beyond comprehension. While on USO tours, I remember special moments when prayer was offered before our shows. We prayed that God would be uplifted, soldiers encouraged, and protection provided for all the servicemen and women. Before a big concert or event, I often call my pastor so he can pray for me to perform at my best, give my all, and be an inspiration to those who will be listening. And when I am away from home, touring somewhere in the country, I make it a point to pray for my family. I rely on God's protection and direction for all of us. Much attention has been given to Broncos quarterback Tim Tebow for showing his faith publicly. How is that a bad thing? He doesn't pray during interviews nor does he pray to win football games. He is asking his God to allow him to play his best and to give thanks for who he is. He also prays for the safety of all the players. I praise him for his courage to do so, and find it interesting that the media is constantly surprised by his strength and resolve. I'm not!

To deny a teacher or student or anyone the right to ask for God's guidance, protection, and blessing is just insensitive and selfish. This is America, for heaven's sake!

The Pledge of Allegiance Is Next

The Pledge of Allegiance to the flag is the next target on the atheists' agenda. The pledge itself has been around since 1892. The phrase "under God" was added and adopted in 1954 by a Joint Session of Congress, with the expressed public approval of 95 percent of all Americans. Ten years later (around the same time the ban on prayer was initiated), this phrase was challenged in a lawsuit filed by litigants made up mostly of atheists. The 9th Circuit Court of Appeals determined the phrase to be unconstitutional. The Supreme Court, however, overruled the lower court's finding, and for that we should be thankful. The vote was close and the reasons given for overriding the Circuit Court's opinion were based on procedural grounds only. Justice Sandra Day O'Connor wrote that the phrase "under God" was actually meaningless. "Any religious freight the words may have been meant to carry has long since been lost." I sincerely hope that is not a true sentiment of most Americans.

In June of 2002, the CNN Web site reported the following: "Nearly nine in ten Americans believe the phrase 'under God' should remain in the Pledge of Allegiance, and most believe it is acceptable for the government to promote religious expression ... according to a *Newsweek* poll."

It is important to realize that it took only five votes from the Supreme Court Justices to ban school prayer and the use of any religious symbols on public property. Only five judges made those sweeping changes. We were again only five votes away from removing any mention of God in our national pledge to the flag. It didn't matter that 95 percent of Americans approved the phrase—five votes could have changed our Pledge of Allegiance.

This fight will come up again, and the words "under God" could be stricken should five judges deem them to be unconstitutional. Also, it could take only a mere five votes to remove the phrase "In God We Trust" from our currency. This should be a sobering thought for all of us who believe God is an integral part of who we are as a nation.

Can you imagine the founding fathers' reaction today to those who are distorting our constitution? It comes down to two choices really: Is God merely a myth to us as a nation, or not? Is God really dead, as the cover of the April 1966 *Time* magazine purported? We are either who we are morally because of God, or our standards are man-made; we've made our own rules. Do we have a Higher Source, or are we on our own in the world? Our answers to those questions will determine the spiritual future and direction of our country.

A Look at Our Spiritual Heritage

Religious freedom is the very cornerstone of our cherished liberty. It is the very reason the early Pilgrims, the Puritans, and the Catholics came to this country. They came for the purpose of practicing their religious beliefs without threat of censorship or persecution.

Although I appreciate the leadership of George Washington, John Adams, Benjamin Franklin, and other early founding fathers, I especially admire Thomas Jefferson, the author of our beloved Declaration of Independence. Jefferson wrote: "All people are endowed by their Creator with certain unalienable rights, that among these are life, liberty and the pursuit of happiness." Consider the genius of Jefferson to embed this basic truth and faith into the very fabric of a document that states who we are as a nation.

Even during the Civil War, a marching song of the Union army, "The Battle Hymn of the Republic," included these words: "As Christ died to make men holy, let us die to make men free." President Abraham Lincoln would write how he was driven to his knees in prayer often during those dark days because there simply "was nowhere else to go." Every president from Washington to the present has spoken of the strength and guidance granted through prayer and faith.

In their book *How to Raise an American*, authors Myrna Blyth and Chriss Winston include these words written by Theodore Roosevelt: "We want to make our children feel that the mere fact of being Americans makes them better off … this is not to blind us at all to our own shortcomings, we ought steadily to try to correct them, but we have absolutely no grounds to work on if we don't have a firm and ardent Americanism at the bottom of everything."

We have found Bill Bennett's *Book of Virtues* and Lynn Cheney's *America, A Patriotic Primer* to be amazing tools for informing our children about our country's great history, as well as providing interesting stories that inspire self-discipline, compassion, a strong work ethic, responsibility, friendship, courage, perseverance, honesty, loyalty, and faith. These are also our two favorite books to send as gifts when new babies arrive in the families of our friends.

A huge part of Americanism is our spiritual heritage. Yet, for years, there has been a trend to delete any mention of God or Christianity from school textbooks. After the courts outlawed religious symbols, prayer, and any reference to God in public schools, it was a natural progression that He be omitted from having a part in our history. How do we reverse the trend to insure that our children receive an accurate account of our nation's history, which would include our religious heritage? Is this the school's responsibility or the parents' responsibility? *Both!*

American History 101

A patriotic education must begin in the home. In the future, it is going to be even more the responsibility of parents to pass along foundational tenets and beliefs to our children. On a personal note, Kim and I have tried to give our sons a basic knowledge of who we are as a country, where we came from, the special circumstances that brought the Pilgrims here, and why our Christian roots are so integral to our Judeo-Christian society.

I once stayed in the Lincoln bedroom while visiting the White House when George Herbert Walker Bush was president and have enjoyed knowing his son, president George W. Bush as well. My personal friendship with past presidents has solidified for me that traditions and history should be known and guarded.

We have also monitored closely what our sons are being taught at school, the information sources, and tenure of class discussions. We firmly believe that in an effort to be politically correct many institutions, even some who are supposedly "faith-based," have sacrificed our country's own important belief system.

I understand the need for separation of church and state. Certainly no denomination or church should be allowed to set laws and dictate political agendas; that would be too extreme. However, this fundamental element of our society is now used as a catchall excuse to eradicate spiritual life and expression of any kind and that, too, is extreme.

Someone asked me recently about my thoughts on the proposed mosque to be built near the World Trade Center site. That is not a difficult issue for me. I don't think any church, mosque, or temple should be built near or on its grounds. Just like Normandy, it is a grave site, a burial site for thousands who lost their lives. State law should approve what should and should not be allowed in or near that sacred place. The presence of a church or any religious building would detract from the serenity, the commonality of the sacrifice made by victims of every faith who died on 9/11.

I realize, too, that although we live in a nation where Judeo-Christian ethics are its foundation, there have been serious moral failures in the lives of those who are supposed to be our spiritual leaders. Well-known and respected preachers, pastors and, priests have been guilty of fraud, greed, theft, and sexual misconduct. When those who are held to a higher moral standard and accountability fail, what should we tell our children? How do we defend our faith? We tell them that people are not perfect and that we shouldn't make idols of men—they are only men. When we trust men rather than God and look to others for divine guidance instead of seeking the truth for ourselves, we will always be disappointed. Keeping our eyes on God, not people, is essential to maintaining personal integrity and spiritual direction. I'm sure that's the hard part for someone who doesn't know or believe in God.

On Allerton Street in Plymouth, Massachusetts, stands the 81-foot-tall solid granite statue titled "The National Monument to the Forefathers." Work began on the statue around 1859, but it wasn't formally dedicated until 1889. Few Americans know of this beautiful work, which was actually a prototype for the Statue of Liberty in New York Harbor. The main figure at the center and top of the statue is called "Faith"; underneath on four main buttresses are the seated figures, named emblematically: "Freedom," "Morality," "Law," and "Education." "Faith" holds an open Bible in her left hand, while the right hand is uplifted toward heaven.

Engraved on one side of the monument are words written by William Bradford, the second governor of the Plymouth colony, in 1620:

Thus out of small beginnings greater things have been produced
> by His hand that made all things of nothing
> and gives being to all things that are;
> And as one small candle may light a thousand,
> so the light here kindled hath shone unto many,
> yea in some sort to our whole nation;
> Let the glorious name of Jehovah have all praise.
> Only by the grace of God have our small beginnings
become great.

While our courts have been banning any reference to God, prayer, religious symbols...

While judicial decisions are handed down that do not follow the values of most Americans...

While our schools are slowly, yet steadily omitting any mention of God from textbooks...

While the secular left continues to spout that God and religious expression is unsophisticated, old-fashioned...

...we must be adamant about electing men and women who truly represent the majority of Americans. The question, "Does God Still Bless the U.S.A.?" may depend upon whom you ask. I believe the majority of Americans still prefer to be protected by the hand of God.

A maN – Me too!

Thanks for "God Bless the U.S. A."

I am Denise Benjamin, SSgt. Joshua A. Throckmorton's aunt and I am writing you to let you know just how much Lee Greenwood impacted my Joshua.

Josh was killed in action by an IED in Afghanistan on July 5, 2011 when he answered a call for help from another unit under fire. His last post on Facebook was read at his funeral and Lee's song, "God Bless the U.S.A." was posted also. Here is the entry; the last entry made by Joshua on July 4th, the day before his death:

> "I remember hearing this song during the first gulf war with my grandparents. This song, along with them, are what makes me as patriotic as I am today. Unfortunately that patriotism is what's keeping me from enjoying this Independence Day with Leslie and the girls. I hope that everyone enjoys this 4th of July."
>
> —Facebook Post on July 4, 2011 12:25 p.m.,
> Ssgt Joshua Throckmorton

Please see that Lee gets this last post home, the last words from Joshua. These are a hero's last words; the words of a patriot. I thank you for all you do for our men and women who are patriots as Joshua was and is. Thank you, Lee Greenwood for the song that changed a boy into a man.

—Sincerely,
Denise Benjamin
Knoxville, TN

How's the Family?

"As the family goes, so goes the nation and so goes the whole world in which we live."

—Pope John Paul II

My boys have grown into young men seemingly overnight. I see in their eyes the wide-eyed wonder of a world just beginning to open up to them. In the next few years they will explore that world and embrace their places in it. If Kim and I have done our job as parents, our sons will not be afraid to determine for themselves the path God has chosen for them to follow. One thing I hope they remember above all is how we worked hard to always make family our number-one priority.

It is a sobering thought that parents set the course of nations by how they rear their children. But it is undeniably true. The statement made above by Pope John was right. There is not a more important institution than this very basic unit of all society—the family. I have become who I am because I was shaped, encouraged, loved, and influenced by family. I consider my role as husband and father to be the most important role I will ever fill. It means more to me than gold records, a room full of Grammies, or any award the music industry could bestow.

So, how is the American family doing, as an institution? Is it in decline or do we still have strong, vibrant families that form the foundation of our nation? (mixed!)

In this chapter you will get to know my wife, Kim, and our sons, Dalton, sixteen, and Parker, thirteen. We will share a little bit of our personal history and the spiritual principles we have established in our home.

—Lee

★　　★　　★

"Thanks for the Memories," Bob Hope

In 1997 the United States Congress named Bob Hope the first Honorary Veteran in our country's history. When he accepted the honor, Mr. Hope said: "This award means more to me than any other." I still miss this great entertainer who died in 2003, but his contribution to servicemen and women around the globe will never be forgotten.

Bob Hope could not have known that he was the one who set in motion the chain of events that would eventually lead me to the girl of my dreams. The USO Tour of 1988 was the final one in which Bob himself participated. Vic Damone had been scheduled to accompany the group but became ill, so Bob called me about going in his place.

The tour went around the world, 25,000 miles, eight shows in eight days. We were to land for our final show in the Azore Islands. Weather conditions prevented us from landing so our 2 C-141 airplanes turned back to Rota, Spain, where after landing, we put on our full show for the Air Force personnel stationed there. The next day we took off for New York and made contact with the military on the Azore Islands as we flew over, giving them our sincere regrets for skipping that show. Miss USA, Bob Hope, and I all wished them a "Merry Christmas" as the holiday was only a few days away. If we had been able to land, I would have met my future wife, as Kim was in the USO GROUP awaiting a flight home from the Azores. Destiny would finally have her way when we met later on.

Later that same year I would take my own USO tour to Europe and Asia. Our first stop was again in the Philippine Islands where I had been only months before. I went again in 1989, and this time I put together a much larger group. I spoke to Miss USA, Gretchen Polhemus, and invited her to go on the tour. She was willing, but said she would like to have two other titleholders accompany her. The ladies had performed together the previous year for the USO abroad. I wanted to see them together on stage, so while in Washington D.C. that same month, I visited the USO and watched some film of them singing and dancing. They were great. One of them, a strikingly beautiful young woman, Miss Tennessee USA, stole my heart from the beginning. The USO contacted them and the girls all agreed to join us on tour. When they arrived at my warehouse in Nashville for rehearsal and orientation, I couldn't take my eyes off Miss Tennessee USA. Her name was Kim Payne and I immediately fell in love with her.

Kim and I became friends on our USO tour and then shared our first kiss on a hillside overlooking the U. S. Navy's Holy Loch Pier in Scotland. It was magic.

We thought we were alone when two young guys dressed in University of Tennessee Volunteer colors—orange shirts and jackets—showed up shouting, "Go Vols!" out of the blue, ruining my romantic moment.

"Oh, man, not now, guys," I muttered under my breath.

What are the odds, huh?

I was honored to have the opportunity in 1989 to join the USO tour to entertain our men and women in uniform. I was equally honored to work with Lee Greenwood, who was at the height of his country career and on an iconic level to the military. I was immediately impressed with how kind and "down to earth" he was; always generous and courteous to me and the other members of the tour.

On Christmas Eve our group was snowed in at a small airport in Newfoundland. Those hours gave Lee and me an opportunity to share Christmas stories of friends and family. I remember finding him so interesting and compassionate. His love for our country and those who serve in the military was deep and genuine.

Lee tells people he loved me at first sight. I don't know about that, but in the weeks and months following the tour, he did put on the "full court press." I was swept off my feet and clearly had never met anyone like him before.

When I met Lee, he was a non-practicing Christian. I knew he had a history of being raised in church and had a respect and love for God, but his faith was not a vibrant part of his life. Lee knew my love for God and family was very important to me, so during those early weeks of courtship, he joined me at church and I began to see in him a real desire for a personal relationship with God. He also set out to win over each member of my family—which he did quickly.

It has always amazed me how God gave Lee the gift of *"God Bless the U.S.A."* I believe He chose him to write and perform this great song that would literally move the hearts of a nation.

—Kim

The Happiest Day of Our Lives

I married the most beautiful girl in the world in April, 1992. The wedding was held at Scarritt-Bennett Chapel in downtown Nashville across the street from Vanderbilt University. It was a perfect day in April with the sun shining and the flowers all in bloom. We had planned this day together and had reduced the guest list down to two hundred people; all the church would hold. Kim was breathtaking as she entered through the back of the church with her father. I've been on stage to sing for presidents, but I was never that nervous. As she approached the altar, I couldn't believe that in the next hour, she was going to commit her life to me. From the day we met, I was in love with her, and I will *always* be in love with her.

Our wedding day was one of the most beautiful days of my life. Surrounded by our closest friends and family we were married at the gothic Scarritt Bennett Chapel in Nashville on April 11, 1992. It was a gorgeous day. The sun seemed to shine a little brighter, the birds sounded happier, the redbud trees seemed more vibrant—it was a magical day.

Rex Humbard officiated at our wedding. Readers may recall the successful evangelism and television ministry of the Humbard family. To me, though, he was "Uncle Rex," whom I had known my entire life. He led my family to Christ long before I was born, married my parents in 1966, conducted my baby dedication when I was six weeks old, and baptized me when I was twelve. Rex Humbard made an eternal impact on my family and it was a joy to share our wedding day with him. Uncle Rex passed away in 2007.

I remember walking down the aisle and seeing Lee's beaming face, and I knew God had brought us together. Lee still tells me it was the happiest day of his life.

—Kim

Holding Down the Fort

As in any new marriage, there were adjustments to be made. Because of my performance schedule I had to be away from home for extended periods of time. This was especially challenging when our sons arrived. God blessed us with two children: Dalton Lee was born in 1995 and Parker Reid arrived in 1998. I thank God every-day for the privilege of being Kim's husband and the father of our two fine young men. Each day I spend with them is an adventure I wouldn't miss for the world.

It was difficult at times when Lee was away. In the early years of our marriage, even when the boys were young, we traveled with Lee quite often. However, once the boys started school, our lives took on more structure and they became more involved in school activities. We do travel with him throughout the year whenever possible.

Even now, this is one of the most challenging parts about Lee's profession; it often takes him away from us. He has missed some "big" moments, but the boys don't feel sorry for themselves in this regard. They actually feel sorry for their dad when he can't make it back for a school event, a play, a game, or a performance. They realize he is out there making music and working hard for our family.

—Kim

I appreciate Kim's decision to "hold down the fort" for me when I am away. She has done an amazing job of making a warm, beautiful home for us; a refuge where I find peace and harmony. Time spent at home energizes me to do what I need to do. Kim chose to be a stay-at-home mom, but she has business interests and maintains an office in our home. As a director for the Miss Universe Organization in Tennessee, Georgia, and Mississippi, she works with hundreds of outstanding young women each year. She sees her involvement in the organization as a ministry to these young ladies as they pursue personal excellence in every aspect of their lives. They couldn't have a better role model than my wife.

How do I maintain our home and manage other interests effectively? Honestly, some days are better than others. I can get overwhelmed because we are all involved in so many things. That is when I focus on the responsibilities God has placed before me. I am blessed to be the mother of two amazing sons and the wife of a man I love and respect deeply. Outside of my relationship with God, they are the most important priorities of my life.

—Kim

 62

The State of Marriage in the U.S.

When discussing the current state of the American home, we must consider the divorce rate and the number of single-parent homes. Most statistics report that more than half of all marriages end in divorce. These numbers are becoming skewed, however, due to the high number of couples who are choosing to co-habitate rather than marry. Kim and I believe strongly in marriage and the commitment it brings to relationships. There is really no substitute for marriage, for the stability and security it provides for children. Divorce, however and whenever it occurs, is painful for all involved.

> Why do I think my parents have such a good marriage? They genuinely enjoy being together and everyone near them has a good time, too.
>
> —Dalton

> I would never place judgment on those who are divorced. However, it makes me sad. There are situations where divorce truly may be the only option, but the fall-out is always destructive and heartbreaking. My grandparents were married for sixty-seven years; my parents have been married forty-five years. I am thankful for the foundation they have laid for us to build upon.
>
> While Lee tends to be very concerned with the political future of our country, I find my heart is heavy and concerned for the spiritual status of the individual and the family, both of which have direct impact on our country's future. People are disconnected from God, from their spouses, from their families, and even from their own hearts.
>
> I see such a crisis in that almost everyone I know is so busy. And busy doing what? We are running here, running there, crazy frantically searching, gathering stuff to the point of exhaustion, collapsing and getting up just to run the race again—what is the point? The result—I know because I have felt it—disconnected. And the wheels come

off. If Satan cannot get you to sin, he will keep you busy and so distracted that he doesn't care if you sin because your voice and your life become irrelevant.

I feel it is valuable to communicate that while Lee and I have a beautiful marriage, not every day of our life together has been a "walk in the park." We have a very deep and wonderful love for each other, we sincerely enjoy being together, and the very best thing we do together is parent our sons. But, I don't know of any couple married for nineteen years that has not had struggles. A life spent in serving God does not make you exempt to adversity. However, I know what it is like to be protected in the palm of God's hand during a swirling storm. If there is one thing I know for sure, if you're not currently in the middle of a storm, you'd better get "prayed up" because a storm is brewing.

During a particularly difficult struggle, one of my closest friends, Deneen Turner, shared with me a special verse that keeps me grounded: "Suffering produces perseverance; perseverance character, and character, hope. And hope does not disappoint us because God has poured out His love into our hearts" (Romans 5:3-5). Beautiful.

When life presses in, it is crucial to connect with the Father or you risk shutting down your heart and performing your way through life in your sleep. Suffering has a greater purpose if we don't numb out to it and become disconnected. The same storm we wish would never come can help grow us into our destinies. The crisis that Satan planned for destruction can help us become the person we are intended to be. God equips us for the places He is taking us to and is actively involved in the details of our lives.

The enemy is so near-sighted that he doesn't see the big picture. While Satan is sneaky and manipulative, only God is omniscient. However, a lot of truth and value can be discarded during moments of suffering. Satan wants us to believe that we are worthless and there is no master plan. Jesus meets us in the middle of the suffering and will lovingly walk us out of the pain and transform us in the process. I also believe firmly when we emerge from our struggles, when that part of our story is done, we have a responsibility, even an accountability, to encourage others. Undoubtedly, there are others within our sphere of influence that will be, or, are facing the same issues.

My good friend and Bible study leader, author Denise Hildreth Jones, said, "When we refuse to entertain the enemy, we go to a new place with the Father. When the world is most bleak, He is the morning star."

The Giver of life is so extravagantly kind. He doesn't keep us guessing. What a comfort to know God wants us to rest and find peace in Him.

—Kim

Keeping Love Alive—Fanning the Flame

Kim and I work on keeping romance alive in our marriage. I love my sons and I want them to see how much I cherish and respect their mother. It isn't hard; she's a beautiful woman. I send flowers when I sense she needs a pick-me-up. I leave a card on her pillow now and then, just to remind her how valuable she is to me. Kim hides a love note in my luggage for me to find when I'm on the road. We have date nights often and plan several get-away trips just for the two of us during the year. We also talk by phone or through texting several times a day when I'm traveling. I love when she sends me a cute text that lets me know she's thinking about me. It is imperative that couples stay connected in every possible way. I think women appreciate words more than gifts, so I tell my bride often how much I love her.

Kim knows the things that make me smile, so she pours me a glass of wine before dinner and cooks my favorite meal every night when we are home together. We watch football games on television with our sons and enjoy seeing special shows we all like. Our sons play several sports at their academy and we rarely miss a game.

Whenever we are out in public, Kim always wears something she knows I like and holds me close to make me feel secure in her love for me. She really knows how to make me feel special. All in all, the love we share is uncomplicated because we care so much for each other. Through words and actions we remain in touch even when we are apart.

Recently, the two of us were in Big Sky, Montana, for a Wounded Warriors event and I watched Lee as he interacted with these men who are true heroes. I said to him, "You are such a good man." He looked back at me and replied, "Not before I met you." I don't believe that is true, but I am proud that our union has brought Lee peace, stability, and a beautiful love story.

Lee is very romantic and generous with his love. Last year on our wedding anniversary, instead of traveling out of town, we had a two-night getaway in our own beautiful city of Nashville. We stayed at a downtown hotel above the restaurant where we went on our first date. At the exact time of our wedding, Lee had arranged for us to be again at the chapel where we married years before. Once inside, he got down on bended knee and with tears in his eyes, asked if I would marry him all over again. We have built a wonderful life together and our marriage is a treasure we guard and protect.

—Kim

Where Are the Fathers?

I believe the absence of fathers in American homes has a devastating impact. I'm sure statistics would show a huge majority of incarcerated men (and women) did not have good, stable father figures to emulate. I personally did not know my father until I was fourteen years old. I actually didn't know my mother that well, either. However, as mentioned, I was raised by wonderful grandparents who loved me and gave me a stable foundation. Though my father was absent, I never felt sorrow or remorse because my grandfather filled the father role and I am forever grateful. Then, my mom married a great guy, Lewis D'Antonoli. He, too, supported me and showed me the love and concern of a real father. I owe these men so much.

God had a wonderful plan in mind by establishing from the beginning that children should have two parents—a mother and a father. Not only are these two people to fulfill each other's needs, but God instructed them to "be fruitful and multiply." He gave them a joint responsibility to love, nurture, and rear offspring. Our country is only as strong as the family. Marriages may end, but families don't. I recall a statement I heard once: "It matters more what happens in *your* house, than what happens in the White House." I agree.

My dad, Jim Payne, and I continue to have a wonderful relationship. He has been the spiritual leader of our family and is always the life of every party! My brother and I appreciate the strong impact Dad has had on us and on our children. My dad is the "go to" person whenever any crisis occurs. He is a godly man who lives out his faith everyday.

I am so grateful that Lee also is having an incredible impact on the lives of our sons. He is their strength, their wisdom, and their buddy. The three of them together crack me up!

—Kim

There are so many things that are special about my father. First, there isn't a mean bone in his body. Others may get angry, but Dad always remains cool and calm. He solves problems with reason and tact, never screaming at people to get things done. Unlike many of my friends, I can go to Dad and talk about any problem or question and he treats me like an equal. He's a great listener. He makes time for me, no matter how busy he is. He respects me and I respect him. I want to emulate my father as I get older, knowing it will make me a better person.

—Dalton

My dad is amazing. Sometimes he's like my pal, joking and playing around together. Other times he's stern and serious when the situation calls for it. There isn't a question I couldn't ask my dad. In fact, he loves it when we go to him for advice. All he asks is that we respect him; that's easy because he deserves it. The most important thing about Dad is the way he loves us; he'd do anything to make us happy.

—Parker

I often pray that I leave my sons a legacy they can build on—one of faith, optimism, and character. Legacy is a powerful thing. Here's the definition: "Something handed down by one who has gone before in the past, and left to those in the present and future." Just to be clear, we *all* will leave a legacy. The question is what kind of legacy we will leave. I think about the impact I will have long after I am laid to rest. Without a doubt, the most important legacy I can leave is to see to it my Christian faith is transferred to our children.

Passing Faith Along

It is profoundly important to me for our children to not only know about God, but to *know* God. I believe with all my heart when our sons leave home for college, they may be academic, athletic, and/or artistic rock stars, but if they do not have a personal relationship with their Creator, I would have failed as a mother. Ultimately, leading our sons to know Christ personally is the most important job I am called to do as a mother.

What a beautiful concept to think about not just respecting and ritualistically observing a deity, but actually knowing God. How humbling to realize that the Creator of the universe desires a relationship, indeed a friendship, with each of us. God didn't create people for religion, but for relationship. Knowing God comes through the privilege of experiencing Him (see Philippians 3:8). It is the desite of my heart that my children always know how to experience God.

—Kim

Kim and I pray in our home, we read and study the Bible, and we take our sons to church. We don't have to force Dalton and Parker to attend church. It is just something we have always done as a family. We believe they understand the value of living good, wholesome, Christ-centered lives. I am so thankful that our boys have experienced the spiritual intimacy that I missed in my early years. The world will try to pull them in all directions but we have given them the compass, the guide to find their way through any situation.

> My faith has proved integral in the decisions I make everyday. It helps me avoid temptation that would lead to serious consequences like alcohol, drugs, smoking, etc. I have been taught to believe my body is a temple dedicated to the Lord and I want to honor God by the way I take care of it. I appreciate the fact that Mom and Dad have laid a spiritual foundation for me and my brother. Many of my friends do not know where to turn or what to do when they are hurt, confused, or feeling peer pressure. I'm thankful for Christian parents, our church, and caring people who believe in me and pray for me.
>
> —Dalton

> My parents have taught me right from wrong. They have also insisted that I choose my friends carefully. I know that my choices, even at my age, could impact the rest of my life. There are lots of opportunities to give in to peer pressure, but I feel so lucky to have parents who understand and a great church support group as well.
>
> —Parker

When Parker was about three years old, he asked Kim, "Who is the guy in the sky that makes me think things?" It brought tears to Kim's eyes because of the unique moment it presented to celebrate Parker's individuality and exactly who he is. Watching our children find their own gifts and talents is exciting and fun! God has a unique plan for them and we feel blessed to be part of the adventure.

> I come from an incredibly good family and am very aware that I stand on the shoulders of great people who have gone before me. The values of my family are very simple: God first, family second, and love for country third. I want to instill those principles into my children, but I haven't had to "force feed" those principles to Dalton and Parker. It is just the "way we roll," so to speak. They get it, and I am so grateful.
>
> —Kim

Growing Up Greenwood

> I have to tell most of my friends how famous my dad is because he's not that famous among kids. (Sorry, Dad!) When most people discover I'm the son of Lee Greenwood, the music artist and songwriter, they are impressed, but then they get to know us and see how we are just a normal family, and I'm just a normal kid. I like it that way.
>
> —Parker

> Most of my friends are very aware that my father is Lee Greenwood. There is a definite positive side to having a famous father; it is an effective icebreaker for example. I get a lot of respect from my friends who are musicians because they recognize Dad's songs and his musical contributions to the country. Dad's celebrity may intimidate some people at first, but he is so friendly and genuine that most of my friends soon see him as "just Dalton's dad." I am very proud of my dad and love him like…well, like a father, of course.
>
> —Dalton

Living normal lives is perhaps one of the most intentional things we do as a family, and I have to say, we do it well! First of all, we don't find ourselves to be all that important. We live life just like everyone else. We stay focused on what is important: God, family, and country. While we are extremely proud of Lee and all that he has accomplished, our family respects the hard work and discipline of our neighbors, the teachers who invest in our children, our pastor and the church staff, the parents of our children's friends. Lee has a somewhat different job, that's all. I think the key is that we just don't take ourselves too seriously.

—Kim

I haven't thought that much about what I will do for a career. I've always dreamed of being a singer like Dad, or perhaps an actor. But, I know everyone wants to be a superstar and some of our dreams aren't realistic. So, I may consider other careers: a lawyer, teacher, or possibly an author. I have plenty of time to discover what I would enjoy.

—Parker

I still have a while to think about a career path, but right now, I tend to lean toward a career that is science related. Perhaps I would enjoy being a doctor; the research would be so exciting! For example, how cool it would be to develop breakthroughs in artificial intelligence.

I'm asked often about following in Dad's footsteps in entertainment. Truth is, I don't have the same musical talent as Dad, but I recently performed with our school's Chamber Choir at Carnegie Hall and that was awesome. (How about that, Dad? You and I both have performed at Carnegie Hall!) Throughout our lives, Dad and Mom have made it clear to my brother and me that we have to follow our own drumbeat and I know my parents will continue to offer guidance and support for both us all along the way.

—Dalton

Mom and Dad make sure we keep family traditions alive. Holidays are special, birthdays always celebrated, and we take many family vacations through the year. I love our Sunday traditions most. Before church, Mom makes cinnamon rolls for breakfast. Then, after church, we often go to a favorite restaurant for lunch.

—Parker

Christmas traditions are important to our family. We put up the Christmas tree and decorate it together (while listening to Dad's Christmas CDs, of course). Many of our family traditions I hope to continue when I have a family one day. Above all, I will make sure God has a place of priority in my home. I will pray for my children just like Mom and Dad pray for us.

—Dalton

Red, White, and Blue Family

We have raised our sons to appreciate our great country. They have traveled enough around the world to know how blessed we are to have the resources, opportunities, and freedoms we enjoy. We continue to teach them to be grateful they were born in America.

I came of age when Ronald Reagan was president. From the ages of twelve to twenty years old, he was my president and it was such an optimistic time. Reagan made everything seem possible. Lee performed with President Reagan at over fifty events. I personally met him on his 80th birthday. It was one of the few speechless moments of my life. Years later, we were honored to attend his funeral and most recently to celebrate his centennial birthday at the Reagan Library. It was moving to hear former Senator Fred Thompson comment, "No Ronald Reagan event would be complete without Lee Greenwood."

We are unashamedly proud of our country. I have traveled the world and found our young country to be extraordinary in so many ways. We are especially proud of our servicemen and women who sacrifice so much to maintain our freedom.

—Kim

I was only three years old when the World Trade Center was attacked in New York City. Our country has been at war in places like Iraq and Afghanistan for most of my life. I won't say I understand all that is happening politically around the world, but I've been taught to respect, honor, and love our country at all times. I've watched my dad perform, *"God Bless the U.S.A."* many times and each time I'm touched by the emotion of the audience. I never get tired of hearing or seeing veterans embrace my dad and thank him for performing, or for writing this special song that means so much.

—Parker

Many of my friends appreciate the freedoms that America offers and consider themselves to be patriotic. Although not everyone agrees with the policies of the president all the time, the institution and system of government is respected and admired instinctively. Like me, most of my friends are not eligible to vote as yet, so the political interest is limited. However, I have a few friends very active in following politics and nationwide trends in business and economics.

I love our country on a level difficult to express. It has been meaningful for me personally to see the impact my father's efforts and his music has made on people of all ages. Dad's words in song have defined for millions what it means to be an American. I have grown up appreciating greatly the sacrifice of our men and women in the armed forces who assure my freedom everyday.

—Dalton

 73

In 2005 a poll taken by Fox News revealed that one out of four young Americans under the age of thirty, would prefer living in another country. Surprising? Another poll that focused on those over thirty had a different result; 95 percent over the age of thirty chose to live in the United States. Still, it's shocking that a quarter of our youth—those who will be charged with maintaining the fight against terrorism, electing leaders, building our economy, raising children—would rather be somewhere else.

Another poll questioned students, grades 1 though 8, about their desire to be president of the United States. Are you ready for this? Eighty percent said, "No thanks." They were simply not interested in the most important job in the world. Our youngsters are growing up in a nation where any man can better himself, become a true statesman, and then rise to take the highest office in the land, yet the majority would not be interested. Have they seen too much of the seamy side of politics and not the value of our great system of government? Do these young people believe the job doesn't make a difference in the lives of citizens, no matter who is in office?

We must teach our children what this nation means. They have to learn about George Washington's character, Thomas Jefferson's intelligence, James Madison's extensive knowledge. They have to hear again and again the stories of the men and women who founded this nation; their thoughts, their aspirations. They must know who Frederick Douglas was and Susan B. Anthony. Do they understand the impact Martin Luther King had on our country? Do our children, deep down, love this country and what it stands for? It is not only our responsibility as parents, it is crucial to our nation's future to teach our children to love, respect, and understand all it means to be an American.

Clara Barton, the Civil War nurse, was also a teacher and humanitarian, and the founder of the American Red Cross. Her statement below is one I pray my sons will one day claim as their own,

"The patriot blood of my father was born in my veins."

There is no greater gift we can give our children—no greater heritage than faith and patriotism.

Thanks for "God Bless the U.S. A."

Hi Lee,

I am the teacher who recently met you and your son. I had sent up a prayer that one day I would be able to tell you in person how much your song, "God Bless the U.S.A." means to all of us at Dr. W. J. Creel Elementary School in Melbourne, Florida. We sing it each Friday and it touches my heart each time to hear the children's voices raised in song! Their favorite part is the chorus, "and I'd gladly stand up next to you and defend her still today (with emphasis on the *"stand up"*)! Perhaps we can send you a video of some of the children singing.

Thank you for offering to send me a signed picture and a C.D. for our school! That was such a kind offer and we would love it! I called my principal, Kathy Eward, and told her I had met you. She asked if I told you how famous you are at our school. She was hoping I would bring you back to Melbourne with me! I told her you were on your way to sing at the California State Fair. We would **love** to have you visit us anytime. So thank you for your kindness and allowing me to share with you. You are one of the "good guys." God bless and keep you and yours.

—Laynie Fulton, Transitional
Kindergarten/First Grade Teacher
Dr. W. J. Creel Elementary School, Melbourne, FL

Bashing America is "In"

Every Muslim, from the moment they realize the distinction in their hearts, hates Americans, hates Jews and hates Christians. For as long as I can remember, I have felt hatred and animosity for Americans.

—Osama bin Laden, *"Messages to the World"*

Hatred is never simply one-way traffic. It is a relational, reactive condition. It affects how judgments are made on both sides of a mutual divide of distrust.

—Ziuddin Sardar
Author, *Why Do People Hate America*

I view them with contempt that grows stronger everyday. I am talking about the United States and Great Britain.

—Harold Pinter, playwright
2005 Nobel Laureate

I grew up believing that our country was good at its core and other nations of the world admired us, even respected us. Call me naïve, but back then I assumed the world viewed us as a shining example of democracy and benevolence. Was I wrong? At the end of World War II, we had just saved the world from the Nazi scourge and from Japan's push for world domination. Weren't we heroes? Victors? Saviors?

Then came the period of the Cold War when the United States was posturing with Khrushchev, the leader of the Soviet Union, over nuclear test ban treaties; the fear of nuclear war was very real. Beginning in the 1950s, families built and stocked bomb shelters and I remember the "duck and cover" civil defense drills in school. We were told that, if and when we saw a big flash of light, to stop what we were doing, immediately get on the ground under something (like a table or desk), and assume the fetal position, covering our heads with our hands. Looking back, it is sort of funny that we believed a simple "duck and cover" drill would protect anyone during an all-out nuclear attack. Those were scary times. No one could have foreseen the eventual fall of the once powerful Soviet Union in our lifetime.

Next came Korea and then the Vietnam War. It was the Vietnam War that deeply divided our country and, for the first time in our history, young men were asking, "Do I have a choice to fight or not?" Like the war in Korea, the war was actually not against the Vietnamese, but against communist aggression. The jungle warfare in Vietnam would be similar to Korea, also, and with a similar result—no clear victory. There were widespread protests of the war in Vietnam on every college campus in the country, and I could surely sympathize with the protesters. They took it too far, however, by blaming our men and women in the military who were just doing their duty—fulfilling vows taken to defend and serve our nation and our president.

My loyalty to country was very strong, and I tried to join the Marines during the Vietnam conflict, but was not selected due to having small children from a previous marriage at the time. My father, Eugene, joined the Navy after the bombing of Pearl Harbor and served on the Liberty ship, "Yugoslavia," during World War II. My stepfather, Louis D'Antonoli, served in the Air Force with his two brothers. I was disappointed that I couldn't defend my country in the same way. But after being rejected by the military, I knew I could be a patriot at home, too.

President George W. Bush declared "war against terrorism" following the tragic events of September 11, 2001. Our young men and women are still fighting that war in the mountains of Pakistan and Afghanistan. The enemy in this war is different. Terrorism is an enemy that knows no country, but exists wherever it is formed and nurtured by hatred. A terrorist could be lurking in any country of the world, even next door. It saddens me to think my sons face a future with an enemy of this sort, an enemy who will not stop until the whole world says, "Enough!" So many children in the world live their entire lives in fear, struggling daily to survive. I am thankful for the joy I see in my sons' faces and pray that nothing will ever steal it away.

As the war continues, it seems that the America-bashing rhetoric has been turned up even more in recent years, and I can't help but wonder where that road is leading. Other nations openly criticize our foreign policy while the Constitution guarantees our own citizens the right to speak against, protest, and even defy our government.

Should the day ever come when America must stand alone and fight terrorism, my hope and prayer is that our leaders and our people are given the wisdom and strength to endure and be victorious, with or without the support of the rest of the world.

—Lee

As the Vietnam War came to an agonizing halt, the world view of America was changing. Some around the world now portrayed her as the aggressor, the bully who arrogantly claimed the role as "policemen of the world." Most of our former allies remained supportive, especially Britain, but some countries backed away and seemed to feel that America was "throwing her weight around" where it was not wanted or needed. Our motives were being questioned on several fronts.

Our Support of Israel

"Israel has no better friend than America. And America has no better friend than Israel. We stand together to defend democracy. We stand together to advance peace. We stand together to fight terrorism. In an unstable Middle East, Israel is the one anchor of stability. In a region of shifting alliances, Israel is America's unwavering ally. Israel has always been pro-American. Israel will always be pro-American," so declared Prime Minister Netanyahu in an address to a special Joint Session of Congress in May of 2011, when U.S. representatives interrupted around thirty times with thunderous applause and standing ovations.

In this post 9/11 era, Israel is a strategic ally and partner of the United States. Israel provides priceless intelligence regarding our mutual enemies, helps U.S. Armed Forces train for and respond to terrorist threats, and supports measures that ensures our homeland security. Israel's military strength is unsurpassed and their partnership is key to stabilizing the Middle East.

Surrounded by hostile neighbors determined "to wipe her off the map," the tiny nation of Israel simply wants to be free from tyranny and savage attacks by those who hate the Jews. Like Americans, they want to live in their own homeland to enjoy family, country, and the expression of their faith. They are industrious, resourceful, and amazingly resilient and a people hoping for peace. Throughout their long history, Israel has rebounded from many wars. Threats of war have forced them to make numerous concessions to their enemies, but they insist on the right to remain in the land of their forefathers and to defend themselves. Incidentally, Israel is the only nation on earth for whom God Himself has set the boundaries (see Numbers 34:1-12). Not only that, but He has declared that this land belongs to Him (see Leviticus 25:23 which states, "The land shall not be sold permanently, for the land is Mine.")

Throughout the Bible are explicit promises and commands that are to be taken very seriously. Sometimes the promise goes hand in hand with the command. One of these is found in the first book of the Bible, when the Lord said to Abraham, father of the Israelites:

> *I will make you a great nation;*
> I will bless you
> And make your name great;
> *And you shall be a blessing.*
> I will bless those who bless you,
> And I will curse him who curses you;
> *And in you all the families*
> of the earth shall be blessed.
> —Genesis 12:3, 4

If we want God to bless the U.S.A., perhaps we'd better take Him at His Word and continue to stand up for Israel. Our ties with her are time-honored. It was Sid Roth, a Jewish rabbi, who reminded us in a recent newsletter that George Washington in his Inaugural Address, delivered at Federal Hall in New York City, declared that American prosperity and protection were dependent upon honoring God as a nation. Later, political leaders of his day gathered at St. Paul's Chapel to commit this nation's future to God and His purposes. That chapel, located at Ground Zero, survived the 9/11 terrorist attack on the Twin Towers, virtually unscathed! Let us pray that our commitment to God, to Israel, and to His land will also remain rock-solid. May we never betray our loyal friends.

Foreign Policy Questioned

None of our past confrontations, wars, or standing in the world community prepared us for September 11, 2001. Didn't it seem like we had the support of every nation following the destruction of the World Trade Center in New York? Yes, for maybe twenty-four hours. Then, it was back to America-bashing.

Author John Gibson writes about a French politician who referred to the 9/11/01 attacks this way: "America brought it on themselves." There were other comments: "Why are Americans who die somehow more valuable than those who die in other countries; and "America had it coming due to their flawed foreign policies around the world."

I must add here that Kim and I have traveled around the world, and have never encountered any personal animosity as American citizens. I do believe, however there are factions in every country that envy and despise us.

After 9/11/01, I was proud and comforted by President Bush who vowed to track down those responsible for taking American lives. If you recall, the president said we would also go after "anyone (or any nation) *harboring* terrorists." He wanted other nations to know we were serious about fighting terrorism wherever it existed. How far do you let a bully go until you confront him or challenge him? How far do you go to avoid conflict? Do you keep the peace at any cost? There are times to tolerate some acts, and then there are times to make a stand, defend, and protect ourselves. That was a time we had to fight back.

On October 7, 2001, I was scheduled to perform "God Bless the U.S.A." and the "National Anthem" prior to the NASCAR race at Charlotte Motorspeedway. I was standing on the track in front of approximately 150,000 people. The television director was counting us down to air time. Seconds before we went to live television on NBC, the director seemed confused and gave me the "stop" signal with his hand. Everything went still. Drivers stood outside their cars in anticipation of the singing of the National Anthem. The fans were also standing in silence. My heart began to race as the seconds ticked by.

Suddenly the large jumbotron in the center of the track which would carry our performance live was interrupted by live footage of America's first attack in the war on terror. As the bombs fell on Baghdad the crowd erupted in thunderous applause. Tom Brokaw appeared on the screen announcing, "America strikes back." The red-blooded Americans at Charlotte Motorspeedway knew that America was finally responding to 9/11/01. Moments later, it would be confirmed that U.S. Armed Forces had launched Operation Enduring Freedom, which was well received by the NASCAR fans. Then my countdown came again. I stood a little prouder, my eyes glistening with tears. I knew our young men and women were in harm's way, but they were defending our country and our freedoms as they had been trained to do.

After the attack, Americans for the first time began to learn the meaning of such words as *al-Qaeda, fatah, hamas, jihad,* and their importance to Islam, Muslim, and Arab factions.

I wonder at times if Americans underestimate the "call to jihad." The word means "holy war." As a Christian, I don't see anything holy about it.

Some say we must diplomatically engage our terrorist enemies. We must address their grievances and try to placate them as much as possible. How can we possibly do this when their main grievance *No* is our very existence, our freedom of religion, our democratic process? They believe we need to be destroyed if we do not embrace and follow the one "true" religion, Islam. In other words, only conversion to their religion can save us. *No!*

In one of the books directed at encouraging and directing acts of violence against Jews and Americans—M*editations on the Jihadist Movement*—these statements are made in a chapter entitled "Small Groups Could Frighten the Americans:"

"Tracking down Americans and Jews is not impossible. Killing them with a single bullet, a stab, or device made up of a popular mix of explosives, or hitting them with an iron rod is not impossible. Burning down their property with Molotov cocktails is not a difficult task either. With any available means, small groups could prove to be a frightening horror for Americans and Jews."

The frustrating detail of this particular enemy is that there is no precise central command, no one leader over all. The terrorists appear to have many leaders and acts of violence may be planned and carried out by one person—a "lone wolf" like Richard Reid, the British-born, al-Qaeda-trained "shoe bomber," who tried to light a match to explosives hidden in his shoe on a flight from Paris to Miami. This incident led to a policy requiring all airline passengers to remove their shoes for inspection before boarding flights. These kinds of attempts are meant to instill fear and to intimidate us because they could literally come from anyone, anytime.

The enemy we face is one who does not hesitate to kidnap Americans (and others) and film their beheading for the world to view via the Internet. They feel justified in encouraging suicide bombers who kill many of their own to promote their cause and gain "glorious martyrdom" status. I wonder how they feel about killing their own Muslim brothers who are Americans? For the suicide bomber, there is a promise of a Paradise which will grant him instantaneous forgiveness of sins, the right to plead for seventy-two other relatives, and seventy-two virgins to service him in heaven. He is more than convinced that giving his life is worth it. Their secondary goal is to create fear and to invoke response and hostility. The American mind-set with our philosophies and values cannot understand this kind of extreme hatred or behavior.

Although I hope the war will end soon and American troops can return home, I understand how important it is to find the cells of terrorism that are planning events like 9/11/01. With the elimination of bin Laden by the Navy Seal team in Pakistan, we have put the terrorists on notice that America is fulfilling the president's promise to hunt down those who would carry out attacks on our country. My family and I pray every night for our military and their families as they sacrifice to protect and guard our freedom.

America: Not Perfect, But Exceptional

Is America exceptional? If we are, why are we so afraid to say so? Because the rest of the world has a problem with America *thinking* we are exceptional. The idea that we believe we are somehow special rubs the rest of the world the wrong way. In my opinion, every citizen of *every* country should believe their country and its people are the best in the world, that's nothing more than national pride. Yet, when we express this concept about America, we are bashed for being arrogant, condescending, or ignorant.

I was intrigued a few weeks ago by an article by Kathleen Parker in the *Washington Post.* She raised the question whether America was exceptional or not when she asked: "Is there something about our country that makes us unique in the world?"

Of course, there are many things that make us unique. First of all, I wonder if most Americans believe we are special? According to the same Parker article, a Gallop Poll revealed that 90 percent of Americans believe Ronald Reagan's declaration: "The United States of America has a unique character that makes it the greatest country in the world." I believe that as well. However, we are not perfect. Our democracy has to evolve with each generation.

Granted, referring to ourselves as "exceptional" at this point in history is problematic for some. After all, we are in the middle of ongoing financial woes, we are engaged in a war with mounting casualties, we have staggering debt and deficits that threaten the future of generations to come. No, we are not perfect, and it certainly may be inappropriate in these "global" times to be egotistical about our world standing. We were, after all, raised with the notion that we shouldn't "brag." It's like a good football team; they don't have to remind everyone of their greatness, they just go out and prove it on the field at game time. America should be the same. We don't have to continually remind the world how great we are; we just need to be great.

There is, however, nothing wrong with national pride; not a swagger, but a healthy confidence, a "knowing" that we are citizens of a unique, beautiful, and blessed country unlike any in the world. We want our leaders, and especially our president not only to believe it, but not to be afraid to say it!

I have met countless veterans who have served in the military, and each one of them comments on their love and pride for our country.

The bashing of America will continue, from without and within. There are plenty of areas where we need reform and real change. The right to peacefully assemble and protest any cause or concern in our government is guaranteed by our Constitution. There are some in America who feel that talk shows go too far in criticism of our government. But that is part of what makes America great. Free speech gives us the right to voice our approval or disapproval. Censorship is not an option. People have a choice. It is the right of every citizen to listen or not to listen, to agree or disagree.

The protesters of the Vietnam War were often greeted with a phrase that has become well-used over the years: "America—love it or leave it." There are many Americans who have that same sentiment regarding our fight against terrorism. War is never good and the sacrifice is always great. The only definition of a patriot is to love America and to be loyal to her.

When the world looks at us, they should see a people founded securely on the principles that established our nation. They should see a people who love and cherish America so much, that even with her faults, they believe her to be the best, the greatest and finest example of charity, democracy, and fairness in the world. Unfortunately, that is not always the case.

A member of the Egyptian Parliament, Mahmoud Shazli, voiced his opinion of America: "The message is, we really hate you. Go to hell with your own fake civilization."

One British author, M. Drabble, wrote: "I loathe America for what it has done to Iraq and the rest of the helpless world."

A Canadian parliament member and others agreed that "our air of superiority will prove to be our downfall."

Do we ignore such anti-American rhetoric? Do we change our policies and philosophies to suit world opinion? What should be our response?

I wrote this brief article for *American Legion* Magazine last year and believe it to be an appropriate response to our country's critics:

What's Right about America

When you look at America as I do and not through the media, you see bright-eyed children who only see the future. They don't look back; they see the world through optimistic eyes. Sure, children everywhere have that attitude, but only here do they have a chance to dream about who they can become—a dream without boundaries. You don't have to be wealthy to have freedom. Our Constitution guarantees it! Our military ensures it!

This land called America exists because those before us got it right. They did a good job of leveling the playing field, leveraging power, and giving every single citizen the same opportunity to have a better life. We as a nation have many challenges ahead, but I'll bet on us—as long as we keep faith and a strong defense, and remember that our neighbor is most likely a veteran!

Thanks for "God Bless the U.S. A."

Mr. Greenwood:

My name is Melissa Gordon and I am an Immigration Services Officer for the United States Citizenship & Immigration Service (Department of Homeland Security).

Part of my job involves adjudicating citizenship applications (N-400's) and then officiating/administrating at Naturalization Oath ceremonies. As you know, during each ceremony, we play a video with your song, "God Bless the U.S.A." I cry each time we play the video/song…each and every time, four times a month (at least). The good folks at the ELKS club provide flags and our newest citizens wave Ol' Glory and sing.

Not only do I get to play a small part in this wonderful moment, but I get paid! I want you to know how much your song means to me and how it elevates my job and my life.

Times ARE tough, but I can't believe how fortunate I am to be an American and hope that I add to others as well. Again, thank you so much for writing and sharing this song and I wish you and yours only the best that life and God has to offer.

—My best for you and your family,
Melissa S. Gordon
Las Vegas, NV

Is America Still the Land of Opportunity?

How's this for an American success story?

A privileged California kid fell into music because it was an easy road. He became an overnight success.

Yep, that's a great story, but it isn't my success story. First, I was *not* a privileged kid. My basic needs were met, but that is just about it; everything else, I had to work for—and work hard. Life on my grandparents' farm taught me responsibility, honesty, and the value of a dollar. I am grateful for those years, but it was anything but easy. I will say, however, that as long as I was busy—-and that was most of the time—I didn't notice I was working so hard.

No trained professionals helped me learn music in my early years. My mother taught me basic chords, but I taught myself to play the piano by ear. The first song I learned by note on the piano was Stan Kenton's "Artistry of Rhythm." I was given an alto sax that had belonged to my uncle and learned to play it as well. I was around thirteen years old when I began to sing in the First Baptist Church in North Sacramento which helped develop my voice. My music teacher in high school, Fred Cooper, encouraged me to learn to read music and introduced me to music theory—thanks, Mr. Cooper.

Music was not all I wanted to do. I loved sports, especially base-ball. However, my grandparents decided to send me to summer school to learn to play the saxophone. After the first lesson, I put my baseball mitt in my sax case and rode my bicycle to the ballpark instead. I continued to do that all summer. Since I improved on the sax, the folks never knew I wasn't taking lessons. I was a runner as well. After working nights playing gigs—usually not getting home until after 2 A.M.—I would get up and go to school at 7 A.M. and run laps around the basketball standards outside before my gym class, which was always first period. My farm chores and my over-pro-tective grandparents kept me home when most kids were involved with organized sports. Music was the only thing they pushed me toward—for which I'm grateful now.

As for making a lot of money? I suppose I was making more than most kids my age. I would be paid anywhere from $5 to $25 a night, playing in some nearby dance hall or night club. We played in a lot of dives, too. While other teens were going on dates, seeing movies, and living it up, I was doing the entertaining. The band leaders I played for had to promise my grandmother that they would protect me and bring me safely home every night. They also had to make sure I was home one hour after we finished playing. That gave us time to get a bite to eat at the all-night diner. They did a pretty good job for the most part, but we dealt with some really rough crowds at times. I never smoked, hated the taste of alcohol, and was never caught up in drugs of any kind. You might think that was some sort of a miracle given the environment I was introduced to at such an early age, but my only interest was the music. It never crossed my mind to drink or smoke.

My overnight success? Let's see, figuring it all up, it was thou-sands of nights over a period of many years before I considered my career a success! The Las Vegas stints alone were tough but exciting. Sometimes I'd work two or three gigs on the same night. I once played piano bar in Montana six hours a night, six days a week for three weeks. I lost my voice completely during that period and had to chase down the manager every payday; he never once paid me on time.

Living in Los Angeles was really expensive, especially with no job. During my time there, I had my car repossessed and sold everything I owned—my shotguns, encyclopedias, and even my saxophones (boy, did that hurt!)—just to pay the rent. My success did not come easily or quickly. There were many years of sacrifice and taking chances. There was no American Idol show to enter that would put me on a fast track to success. It was hard work, but I figured it was worth every late-night honky-tonk to get to where I needed to go.

I wrote many songs before I wrote the song I am best known for. For every hit I've had on radio, there were twenty or more that never even made it to the recording studio. Songwriters are usually working on many songs at once, but they may have only one song in a lifetime that makes it to the charts and is recognized as a true hit. I've been blessed to have thirty or more hits, but "God Bless the U.S.A." has become my signature song. After years of putting words and music to paper, the song came easily. Without a doubt, God guided me through all the tough years just to write that one song.

I still love singing and entertaining. I strive to be artistic and give my all for each performance. My work ethic will not allow me to do less. I am honored that people pay their hard-earned money to come and see me, so I want to make sure they leave satisfied and happy for the moments we spend together. I maintain a busy schedule and I like it that way. However, my road show, personal appearances, rehearsal time, writing this book, PR events and traveling take me away from my wife and sons almost every week of the year for a day or so, and sometimes for weeks at a time. I regret that I have missed so many events in their lives, but they know I am working to provide the best possible life for our family. Kim also works, and her job takes her away several times a year. We often joke about who is home with the kids! Rest assured, they always have family and friends watching over them.

I'm not so naïve as to say America is the only country in the world where one can have the kind of success I enjoy today. But this country was created by determined people who believed that if they worked hard and persevered, great things could be achieved. There may be some who believe America is no longer "the land of opportunity." Not I, and not the thousands who immigrate legally to our country every year. America is still the land of opportunity, and I owe a huge debt of gratitude to this country for taking a chance on a scrawny kid whose dreams took him far beyond what he had ever hoped.

—Lee

★ ★ ★

In New York Harbor stands the Statue of Liberty with the words of a now famous poem engraved on the main entrance. The most recognizable part of the poem implores the world to seek safety, prosperity, and opportunity here in our country.

> Give me your tired, your poor,
> Your huddled masses yearning to breathe free,
> The wretched refuse of your teeming shores.
> Send these, the homeless, tempest-tossed to me.
> I lift my lamp beside the golden door.
> —from "The New Colossus" by Emma Lazarus

Written in 1883, the poem was not discovered until after the author's death at 37 years of age. Emma Lazarus, a young Jewish woman from a privileged family, was passionate about the plight of Jewish people around the world who were suffering persecution. Her poem reflected their struggle for freedom. A woman, organizing fund-raising events for the erection of the statue, found the poem tucked underneath many other papers and old letters. Touched by its words, she led the effort to make sure Emma's poem appeared alongside the Statue of Liberty forever.

My English and Irish ancestors, along with many others, took Lady Liberty up on her invitation to come to America. Thousands came from around the world to build a better life. What they found was anything but an easy road to wealth and security. Quality housing was unavailable, so they lived in tiny, cramped apartments. Those who found work toiled for long hours under deplorable conditions. Men, women, and even children worked for little pay in filthy, unventilated factories. Because of overcrowding and lack of clean water, disease was widespread in the New York slums where most immigrants lived. Not exactly the end of the rainbow many had expected.

Yet, this is America's heritage. Even our beginnings were born out of revolution and the yearning to be truly free. This made us a stronger, more determined people. We are a nation made up of European immigrants who bought into the American dream—the dream described in our Constitution as the right of *everyone* to "life, liberty and the pursuit of happiness."

The immigrants who helped build this nation and other hard workers from "The Greatest Generation" like my grandfather, Tommy Jackson, and my wife's grandfather, Lindsey Payne, cherished their citizenship. Here they knew they were free to follow their dreams—whatever those dreams happened to be. Many of our country's most successful companies were started by the hardy men and women who came to forge out a living in this new land. There is not enough time or space in this book to recount all the great success stories of Americans who believed in themselves and their dream, but I do want to mention some of my favorite "only-in-America" stories.

Sam's Story

Samuel Moore Walton was born in Kingfisher, Oklahoma, in 1919. When "Sam" was five years old, the family moved to Missouri. As a young boy during the Great Depression, he watched his mom and dad struggle to make ends meet by taking on odd jobs and trading for goods and services the family needed. It was part of his responsibility to help provide for the family. Everyday he milked cows, bottled the surplus with his mother, then delivered the milk to a few local families. He also had a paper route and sold magazine subscriptions.

After graduating from the University of Missouri with a business degree in economics, Sam served in the Army during World War II. Following the war, when he was twenty-six years old, he borrowed $20,000 from his father-in-law to purchase a dime store in Kansas City, Missouri. Sam's sales and business practices led to the store's success and the purchase of three other dime stores in the Midwest. The first Wal-Mart opened in Rogers, Arkansas, in 1962. Sam was determined to market American-made products from American manufacturers at prices low enough to compete with foreign-made products.

To date, there are 8,500 Wal-Mart stores operating in fifteen countries. Sam was named the "Richest Man in America" by *Forbes* magazine during the 1980s, a label he didn't care for after he began to receive hundreds of requests for money. Some of these were legitimate needs. Others were ridiculous, like the woman who said she'd never had a $100,000 home and wondered if he would just buy her one because he had the money.

Sam became a billionaire, but continued to live a simple, frugal life until his death in 1992. He drove around Bentonville, Arkansas, in an old pickup truck, wore a Wal-Mart baseball cap, shopped for his clothes at Wal-Mart, refused to fly first class, and was known for pinching pennies. He became an American folk hero due to his common sense values and homespun approach to customer service. He once stated, "There is only one boss, the customer. And he can fire everybody in the company from the chairman on down, simply by spending his money somewhere else."

Sam Walton and the Walton family have donated millions to charities, schools, and ministry organizations. Sam's impact continues as his business principles are modeled, taught, and studied by would-be entrepreneurs around the world. Sam credited the love of his wife, Helen and their four children, along with the free enterprise system of the United States, for his success.

Sam's story is repeated time and time again by others who believe in the same principles: Work hard, save, and be smart with your money, and you can achieve success in America.

The Disney Dream

On any given day, children and parents alike are whisked away to magical lands where bravery, goodness, and true love always win—a place named for its creator, Disneyland. I think the creation of Disneyland changed the way we perceived entertainment and enhanced the American dream for millions around the world. It became the model for every theme park since—a safe place where children could imagine a fantasy world of villains, princesses, and pirates. The theme park expanded to include additional parks like Disneyworld, Magic Kingdom, and the EPCOT Center, all with the same goal in mind—to delight the inner child in all of us. It all began with one man's American dream.

Walter Elias Disney was born in 1901 and spent the first few years of his life moving from town to town with his family. His father was a builder by trade and had to go where the work happened to be. When Walter was around six years of age, the family bought a farm in Marceline, Missouri, and the memories of life on the farm became a source of inspiration to the young man throughout his career. After attending art school and serving a stint in the military, Disney tried his hand at his own business in Kansas City. It failed miserably and bankruptcy forced him to consider moving to California to join up with his brother, Roy, in a new endeavor. There, in his uncle's shabby garage, Walter and Roy pieced together original illustrations and worked on animation concepts that would revolutionize the movie industry by the 1930s. *Snow White and the Seven Dwarfs*, their first full-length movie cartoon, was hailed as a major breakthrough in film technology and color animation. Many successful projects followed.

Walt Disney's dream was to create a magical place for children, and in 1955, Disneyland opened in Southern California with many dignitaries present for the opening ceremony, including a budding actor by the name of Ronald Reagan. That same year I lived a stone's throw from the new Disneyland theme park. After the park opened I would play saxaphone in a Keystone Kops Quartet, but because of my age I was required to leave the park by ten o'clock each night. From our home on the corner of Ball Road and West Street I could watch the fireworks from Disneyland every night as they exploded almost directly overhead.

Disney's comments on that warm day in July included the following dedication statement: "To all who come to this happy place, welcome. Disneyland is your land. Here age relives fond memories of the past...and here youth may savor the challenge and promise of the future. Disneyland is dedicated to the ideals, the dreams, and the hard facts that have created America...with the hope this be a source of joy and inspiration to all the world."

The creator of lovable creatures from Mickey Mouse to those who live forever in *The Jungle Book*, died at the age of sixty-five, but his dream lives on. Walt Disney not only lived out his dream, but his legacy encourages us to do the same. Imagining a world without Disneyland is like imagining a world without sunshine, hope, adventure, or a child's laughter. I couldn't think of a more appropriate person to include in this section of the book. Walt Disney grabbed hold of the American dream, and we will reap the joy of that dream for generations to come.

Overcomers—The American Way

Some of our country's most successful business executives experienced devastating financial loss before finding something that really worked. (Sound familiar?) Many of our nation's presidents did not come from privileged backgrounds. Six former presidents, including Abraham Lincoln, were born in log cabins. Even a peanut farmer from Georgia came up through the political ranks to become president.

Some of our greatest athletes overcame serious hardships to set records. In 1902, a troubled young boy of seven was sent to a Catholic home for children in Baltimore, Maryland, because he could not be managed at home. He and his sister were the only siblings out of eight that had survived. While staying at the home off and on until he was nearly twenty years old, the boy learned discipline and also learned to love the game of baseball. One of the Catholic brothers, a teacher, invited the manager of the Baltimore Orioles to take a look at the young man's baseball skills. Ernestine Miller described this young player in her book, *The Babe Book: Baseball's Greatest Legend Remembered.* Babe Ruth was nineteen years of age when he was signed to his first baseball contract. The rest, as they say, is history. The Babe rose from a poor, harsh environment to become one of the greatest baseball players in history with a lifetime batting average of .342. He hit 60 homeruns in the 1927 season—a record that stood until 1961 when Roger Maris hit 61.

I can also think of scores of entertainers who grew up in destitute family situations to become widely acclaimed, well-known performers. The "King of Rock 'n Roll," Elvis Presley, was born in a two-room shanty in Tupelo, Mississippi, to parents who barely eked out a living. Country music legend Loretta Lynn's story is also widely known. Only in America could an uneducated coal-miner's daughter from Butcher Holler, Kentucky, be named to Country Music's Hall of Fame and, most recently, awarded the Grammy's Lifetime Achievement Award. Oprah Winfrey overcame poverty, abuse, and racial prejudice to build a television empire and become one of the most influential and powerful women in the world. These examples are typical of people who did it the American way.

Opportunity Comes Knocking

Like thousands of others, I believe I owe my success, in a large part, to being born an American. We all benefit from the unique rights and privileges of a democratic society. These are the same rights and privileges by which my sons can see their own dreams come to fruition. Why do people come here from around the world? Because nowhere else in the world is liberty and freedom offered so broadly. We offer our citizens the best chance to succeed in reaching personal goals. We have the finest educational institutions and a system that focuses on each child's potential and abilities. Our natural resources include coal, oil, and water. Bountiful sources of food and other goods are unparalleled. Most importantly, America guarantees all of her citizens the opportunity to pursue their own dreams, unhindered and unrestricted. How blessed we are to call this wonderful land our home!

One of the reasons we are seen as the "land of opportunity" is found in our distinct, unique culture. Our country was founded on ideals and principles based on moral responsibility. Woven into our basic fabric are values like trust, compassion, courtesy, honesty. These values, I believe, still matter.

The true story of Chris Gardner is another example of someone who took advantage of an opportunity to succeed in the U.S.A. In 1981, the salesman lost everything he had; his car, his home, bank accounts, his credit cards; finally, his wife left him, too. Evicted from his home, he was forced to live for months on the streets with his young son. Eventually, Gardner heard about a training program for becoming a stockbroker, offered by Dean Witter, but it would take six months with no pay! Gardner entered the program and attended the classes, but had to scrounge daily for a few dollars, often selling his blood for money to buy food. He and his young son slept in dirty shelters and train station bathrooms, surviving the best they could. Wearing his one tattered suit, he competed everyday with twenty other candidates for one position.

Actor Will Smith played Chris Gardner in the hit movie, *The Pursuit of Happyness*. At one dramatic point the main character tells his young son, "Hey, don't ever let someone tell you, you can't do something–even me. You got a dream– you got to protect it. Some people can't do something themselves, so they want to tell you that you can't do it. You want something? Go get it—period!" Thousands applauded in theaters coast-to-coast when Gardner earned the coveted stockbroker position and shortly thereafter became a successful self-made millionaire.

There is something inbred in Americans that motivates us to fight harder when our backs are against the wall. Our hardy ancestors, who carved out this land under the harshest of conditions, have passed down DNA that is still evident in the men and women who dare to start new businesses in a challenging economic period. Statistics from Census.gov estimate 600,000 businesses are started each year. The entrepreneurial spirit remains alive and well in our country.

The promise of owning their own piece of ground lured the colonists to our shores generations ago. This hunger for ownership also drew thousands to participate in land-runs in Oklahoma and throughout the Midwest in the latter part of the 1800s. As far as the eye could see, men and women in wagons or on horseback, some even on foot, lined up awaiting the signal. At the sound of the bugle, everyone rushed to claim their own lots, up to 160 acres, and drove down stakes to signify ownership.

We are still driving down stakes today. The ability to own one's own home is the measure most often used for determining individual success. We strive for the privilege of owning our own land, homes, cars, farms, and businesses. Even in a climate of economic uncertainty, this inbred desire for ownership results in Americans turning out the finest products, building on what hard work alone can accomplish, and determining to succeed, no matter the odds. These elements will never change—it is who we are.

Is America's Freedom in Jeopardy?

America's Constitution exists to expand the rights of our people and to limit government. This was the original goal of the framers of this great document. It basically states that our rights come from God; they are "inalienable" rights, which are part of our natural existence, not granted by our government. Pursuing happiness is one of our God-given rights as individuals. So success in America shouldn't depend on a person's economic status, race, or by what the government can do. Success should be measured by two things. The ability to take advantage of our freedom and a person's own level of determination and willingness to sacrifice to reach a goal.

We also benefit from a judicial system of laws and statutes with checks and balances administered by the people. The freedom of speech allows healthy dialogue on issues and guarantees freedom of expression. However, this should not be a license to misrepresent the truth, or to hate or insult others.

We've discussed the importance of freedom of religion in Chapter 3, but I want to reiterate that our country was founded by men who believed in God. As an American, I should have the right to "be religious." I should be able to give thanks, to celebrate Christmas, or to pray when I choose. I can respect the beliefs of others, but I shouldn't have to change mine, or to stop being religious because it may offend someone else. The opportunity we have to worship as we choose is a vital part of our unique identity.

We can travel freely in our country without restriction. We also have the freedom to stay here, or to leave. We can choose to listen to others or to ignore them; to act or not to act. We choose whom we associate with, where we work, and how we live our lives.

Even with the benefits of living in our great country, we know that we are not perfect. Here are some of the concerns:

In the last few years, we have gone from being the largest creditor nation in the world to one of the most indebted.

Drug use, divorce, murder, rape, teen pregnancy, and the number of illegitimate children born every year are on the increase at an alarming rate.

Figures from the Bureau of Labor Statistics show we rank low in work place production, in comparison to the rest of the world. Also, the number of the unemployed continues to rise.

Challenges in literacy and education must be addressed. Test scores of our students should be higher, especially in math and science.

Illegal immigration has increased crime, burdened our health care systems and welfare programs.

Congress continues to debate health care issues while many of those approaching the age to receive Social Security and Medicare benefits wonder if the programs will even survive over the next few years. Add to this the growing concern of caring for millions of "baby boomers" who will be requiring geriatric attention in upcoming decades.

America's ongoing involvement in the war against terrorism claims more lives everyday and new threats in other regions around the world may call for military action, too.

Reclaiming the American Dream

With all of that noted, perhaps we need to be reminded that we have survived tough times before: Depressions, economic upheaval, wars, threat of wars, changing of laws, political and social unrest and terrorist attacks. We are a resilient people who know how to "bounce back." There is a deeply entrenched ethos that will always be part of the American outlook—the pursuit of the American dream. When our country was founded, that dream included free land to the settlers and whatever hard work and frugal living could buy, not "streets of gold" and limitless wealth for the taking that some imagined. Pursuit of the American dream, as referenced in the writings of our forefathers, is the theme in many of our literary classics and, most recently, is the focus of President Obama's book, *The Audacity of Hope: Thoughts on Reclaiming the American Dream.*

So what exactly does the American dream look like today? I suppose the answer depends on how we define "success." If we were to consider what it means to be truly rich, I think perspective on the American dream would change. We would be satisfied with less, we would not be as wasteful, and our goals would not be centered on pursuing material wealth as much as seeking peaceful, meaningful lives.

★ 101 ★

America, for generations to come, will be the land of opportunity because of the "sense of the possible" found here. Writer David Kamp used that phrase in a *Vanity Fair* article, "Rethinking the American Dream." It's true: Most people don't get rich in America, but there is a sense that they are better off, more stable, more likely to make it here. That is why our way of life draws other people to us.

In the same article, Kamp recalled how President Roosevelt encouraged the nation in 1941 when we entered World War II. He spoke of the four freedoms most at stake during that conflict: Freedom of speech, freedom of worship, freedom from want, and freedom from fear. These four freedoms I mentioned when writing the music to "The Pledge of Allegiance." You will find that song on my "America Patriot" album from 1992. Artist Norman Rockwell was inspired by FDR's words and created four poignant scenes of Americans exercising these four freedoms. He chose a tough, barrel-chested man speaking his mind at a town hall meeting to depict the freedom of speech. For the freedom of worship, many will recall the elderly lady sitting in a church pew. For freedom from want, Rockwell's painting of the family preparing to share Thanksgiving Dinner will forever be a much-loved portrait of real "Americana." Lastly, to depict freedom from fear, he chose to paint a young couple peeking in on their sleeping children.

For me, those paintings portray the essence of the American dream and why we will continue to be the "land of opportunity." We offer people the chance for a better, safer life.

In 1963, civil rights leader Martin Luther King delivered his famous "I Have a Dream" speech in front of the Lincoln Memorial in Washington, DC. I was moved also by King's words in a letter he sent from a Birmingham jail that same year:

"We will win our freedom because the sacred heritage of our nation and the eternal will of God are embodied in our echoing demands…When these disinherited children of God sat down at lunch counters they were in reality standing up for what is best in the

American dream and for the most sacred values in our Judeo-Christian heritage, thereby bringing our nation back to those great wells of democracy which were dug deep by the founding fathers in their formulation of the Constitution and the Declaration of Independence."

I hope King's words inspire all of us to embrace the American dream and pursue it with passion and faith. From the beginning, and at every pivotal time in our history, patriots have echoed the same message: The only requirement in this land of opportunity...is the boldness to dream!

Thanks for "God Bless the U.S. A."

Dear Lee,

Our daughter, Rebecca was on the KAL007 plane which the Soviets shot down in 1983. I've just learned that you wrote your most special song, "God Bless the U.S.A." in response to that senseless act.

You have comforted me. Thank you so much.

—Mary Beal,
Mother of Rebecca Beal Scruton,
28 years old at time of death

Seriously, Does My Vote Count?

> Nobody will ever deprive the American people of the right to vote except the American people themselves, and the only way they could do this is by not voting.
>
> —Franklin D. Roosevelt

I was a senior in high school in 1959, the year I served as drum major for our high school band. That year, we were asked to perform at a welcoming ceremony for then Vice President Richard Nixon, who was making a visit to Sacramento. I happened to be one of the first people in line when Nixon stepped off his plane to greet the crowd. I recall how he firmly shook my hand and looked directly into my eyes. I was too young to vote and had no political affiliation, but I knew I was meeting someone important to our country. I had no way of realizing Nixon would later become the President of the United States. I have had the privilege of meeting and performing for several of our country's presidents. I believe theirs is the most important job in the world and respect these men who have been chosen to lead our country, regardless of political party differences.

A little country church down a back road in the small Tennessee town where we live is the site where Kim and I cast our votes for city, state, and national elections. The volunteers manning the polling place are usually senior citizens. Every time we go in, I get a sense they want to pat us on the back—like good children who have completed their homework. I finish my ballot and put it into the electronic counter that tabulates the votes. Then, after peeling off the backing, I place the "I Voted" sticker on my shirt, hoping others will be reminded to vote as well.

As I walk from the school, one of thousands of polling locations across the nation, I think of the price that was paid by patriots throughout history who "gave that right to me." I sense the approval of the thousands of men and women who paid the ultimate sacrifice to assure me this privilege.

I first voted in 1964 when I was twenty-one years old and have not missed voting in a presidential election since. To me, it is one of the most sacred, meaningful opportunities our democracy offers—one we should never take for granted nor neglect.

—Lee

★ ★ ★

When our country was established, the right to vote was tied to the amount of property one owned. The original colonies borrowed this practice from Britain. Their qualification for voting privileges was that a person be twenty-one years of age and own land or possess income worth at least forty shillings a year (approximately $8.60 in 1776). This method, they thought, would ensure that the voter would have a permanent stake in the community and in who or what was being voted on. The thinking was, if you were not competent enough to acquire property of some kind, you probably were not competent to vote.

As relations with England began to deteriorate, the principle of "natural rights" became more and more appealing. The term simply meant there are certain rights that should be afforded to all individuals as human beings—the right to vote being one of them. Benjamin Franklin voiced this opinion in his writings:

Today, a man owns a jackass worth $50 and he is entitled to vote; but before the next election the jackass dies. The man in the mean-

time has become more experienced, has knowledge of the principles of government, and his acquaintances with mankind are more
extensive and he is therefore better qualified to make a proper selection of rulers —but the jackass is dead and the man cannot vote.
Now, gentlemen, pray inform me, in whom is the right of suffrage?
In the man or in the jackass?

With the nation's victory for the War of Independence, the outcry
for extended voting rights continued. Andrew Jackson became the
spearhead for the movement referred to as "Jacksonian Democracy,"
and by 1840 the right to vote for all white male adults was the norm.
After that date, all requirements to own property were dropped.

In 1870, following the Civil War, a new amendment gave non-
white males the right to vote. The vote was still tightly restricted,
however, by poll taxes and tests given to prove competency to vote.
Since many African Americans were former slaves who could neither read nor write, the restrictions made it impossible for them to
vote. This changed as more and more African-Americans became
eligible to vote. Today, they are a vibrant, influential force in our
nation's political process. *Good!*

In 1878 Susan B. Anthony drafted the amendment that would
allow women the right to vote, but it would be forty-two more years
(1920) before this amendment would be added to the Constitution. *Wow!*

The next important change came about when the minimum age
for voting was dropped to eighteen. The debate raged at a time when
many young people were involved in student activism regarding the
Vietnam War. The military requirement for service had already been
dropped to eighteen, and the argument was that if these young men
and women were old enough to be drafted to serve in the military,
they were old enough to vote. The slogan was, "Old Enough to
Fight, Old Enough to Vote." The 26th Amendment was ratified in
1971, giving the right to vote to citizens eighteen years of age.

I remember being excited when eighteen-year-olds were given
the right to vote. It certainly seemed appropriate when young peo-

ple that age were serving, even dying for our country in Vietnam. Eighteen-year-olds may be easily influenced, but kids are getting smarter all the time. Their awareness of issues adds a fresh new vitality to our election process.

The most recent change to voting rights was in 1986, when voting privileges were granted to those in military service serving overseas, aboard ships, and in foreign countries in government service.

Much of the debate these days regarding the voting system in our country seems to center around the legitimacy of the electoral college established in Article II of the Constitution. The number of electoral votes for each state is determined by congressional representation for each state. The larger populated states have more electoral voters, the premise being that whoever wins the popular vote in a state wins all the pledged votes of the state's electors. The popular vote takes place in November; in mid-December, the electoral college (538 citizens) meet to cast their votes. It takes 270 electoral votes to win the presidential election. However, there have been instances in the past in which an elector votes counter to the popular vote, disregarding the choice of the people in his or her state.

Those opposing the electoral college think the election for president and vice president should be determined by the popular vote alone. In the early history of establishing a democratic society, the electoral college had a sensible reason to exist. Now, I'm not so sure. I tend to agree that elections should be determined by the popular vote if a federally controlled system could be adopted that would regulate each state's elections. This would at least eliminate ballot-tampering and inconsistencies of balloting between states.

Getting People to the Polls

Whether or not changes come in the electoral system, there is another more important issue that concerns me: How do we get more of our citizens to the polls? I have heard the comparison noting that more people vote in television's *American Idol* contest than vote for President of the United States. This can't be a relative argument since *Idol* voters can vote more than once.

So...how many people did actually vote in the 2008 presidential election? According to statistics posted by the Web site, Infoplease.com, 56.8 percent of eligible voters voted, or a little more than half our population, a higher percentage than we have seen in several years. The age group showing the most improvement in voter turnout was the 18 to 24-year-old group. In fact, this voting bloc reflects the second highest numbers since 18-year-olds won voting rights in 1971.

It is safe to say, in the presidential election of 2008, Barak Obama appealed to the younger demographic who wanted change. This followed a pattern set by earlier elected presidents who were younger than their respective opponents. President Obama seemed, for some, to be the younger, more energetic candidate. His campaign did a thorough job of focusing on and relating to young people. I am proud of the response of our young citizens who made their voice heard, and I hope the trend continues. It will be interesting to monitor future numbers as the election hype wears off and key issues remain. I think the wave of the future in directing campaigns will be keyed on how to continue to influence and garner the young vote through social networking, Facebook, Twitter, etc. One day we may even be able to vote on-line—now that would be convenient, wouldn't it?

Even with the impressive numbers recently, nearly half of our population still chose not to vote. Several reasons were given: "I didn't have time; I was confused about the candidates; I wasn't informed enough about the issues; politics as usual will not make any difference, no matter who is elected; I didn't like or identify with the candidates." This excuse, however, was the most concerning response: "My one vote won't make a difference."

I want to remind you that there have been incidences in history where only *one* vote has changed the outcome of presidential elections. In 1824 Andrew Jackson won the popular vote. None of the four candidates, however, received an electoral majority, so the election was handed over to the U. S. House of Representatives. In the House John Quincy Adams received one vote more than Jackson to become the nation's 6th president. The process was repeated in 1876, when the House of Representatives elected Rutherford B. Hayes as president—again by one vote.

There are too many examples to cite here, but I encourage the reader to do an Internet search on the importance of one vote—it is eye-opening. Who can forget the "dangling chad" recount in Florida that reiterated the importance of every single vote? The final results confirmed that George W. Bush carried Florida in the 2004 presidential election by only 534 votes. President Bush won New Mexico's race that year by an even closer margin—323 votes!

Voting is a Privilege

With so many countries failing to offer their citizens the option of electing officials, most Americans are aware that voting is a patriotic duty that should be cherished and never taken for granted. Many more countries extend voting rights to men only. In 2005, for the first time in history, Kuwaiti women were given the right to vote and hold office. I recall seeing photos of the women who ventured out in sweltering heat to stand in long lines for the privilege of casting their votes. Many left the voting booths weeping; some exited with huge smiles, then joined other women to celebrate this long-awaited privilege.

Even when America comes to the aid of other countries who desire to establish a democratic society, one of the first designated efforts is to help organize and oversee open and fair elections. We know that nothing speaks of democracy like people choosing their own leaders.

Many immigrants to this country recall with awe the first time they were able to vote as American citizens. One poll worker told me about an incident in San Diego, where the polling place was set up in the garage of a home. Volunteers had placed a small American flag on the check-in table. An Asian-American woman approached the table, stood before the flag for several moments, hand over her heart, and recited the Pledge of Allegiance in a whisper. She then kissed the flag as a sign of devotion to a country that had blessed her with the right to vote. We all need to be that appreciative of this important process of democracy in action.

One of the most enduring examples parents can set is to vote and to teach their children the value of voting. I think it would surprise us to know how many people, who are the most vocal in condemning our government and its leaders, never actually show up at the polls. This reminds me of author Louis L'Amour's statement: "To make democracy work, we must be a nation of participants, not simply observers. One who does not vote has no right to complain." It's like the potluck supper at church. Don't complain about the fare if you didn't bring a dish yourself.

Voting is as patriotic as standing for "The Star Spangled Banner" or remembering our veterans on Memorial Day. It is what true patriots do.

Is Our Political Process Broken?

I think it is safe to assume that most Americans feel there is too much partisan politics. They don't see positive changes or decisions being made because elected politicians spend so much time and energy attacking each other. So far, no one has offered a better way to manage the partisan bickering. It's like an old "damsel-in-distress" movie. Nell is tied to the train tracks, the train is coming, and the two cowboys trying to save her are busy fighting each other. Could our political process be broken?

I don't think it's broken, but it is in need of a few repairs. In my opinion, our two-party system, with the fringe involvement of third-party candidates is healthy for the country. I believe, also, that the division of Senate and House of Representative members is the best way for a democratic system of government to operate. These "checks and balances" can often be exasperating, but at the same time, the interests of the American people are served as we elect those who will represent us best.

As a conservative, I tend to vote for candidates who share my views; however, if my preferred party did not have a candidate in whom I had complete confidence, I would consider the other party's candidate. For most Americans, the choice is usually very clear as to the party with which they most identify.

In 1975 Ronald Reagan delivered a speech encouraging Americans to embrace their unique place in the world, as he called for citizens to reject "pastel colors" (signifying weakness) and choose "the bold colors" of freedom. As he said on many occasions, "We don't need red states or blue states [denoting party participation], as much as we need "red, white, and blue states." He was asking people to perform their civic and patriotic duty, regardless of party affiliation. These are characteristics which led Ronald Reagan to win 49 states in the 1984 election.

It is no secret that there has been a resurgence of voter unrest, the disgruntled public saying, "Enough of politics as usual." I tend to agree. For too long, our political system has favored the special interest groups, bureaucracy, and partisan politics. There have to be solutions both sides can support. It is our responsibility to elect representatives who will put aside partisan politics in favor of solving some of our greatest concerns. The result would be real and lasting change.

Change is needed, but it will be up to us, the voters, to determine the future. The system will only be transformed when our hearts and souls unite to elect men and women who are determined to have the government Lincoln spoke of in his Gettysburg Address: "A government...of the people, by the people, and for the people."

In the same speech, Lincoln went on to declare that this kind of government "shall not perish from the earth." It seems that many of our elected officials favor the paid lobbyists, consultants, bureaucrats, and special interest groups over "the people." The political landscape needs to change.

More than ever, there is a yearning in the nation for the truth. Wouldn't it be refreshing to have someone tell the complete truth about what is working and what isn't working in our domestic and foreign policy? Is there someone who will "tell it like it is" about the inefficient special interest groups, the waste of government spending, and the out-of-control budget? Our country's future depends upon our electing people to do just that—to tell the truth. Voting is important because it puts politicians on notice: "Politics must change, or we will change our politicians."

I was shocked when my sixteen-year-old son Dalton, in all sincerity, asked, "Is the American experiment almost over?" As more changes take place, what's left? Will we still be the America we know, or will we become something different?

In a recent conversation with Newt Gingrich, he made a statement that we believe to be true. "The election of 2012 will be the most important election since 1860."

A Few Needed Changes

With all that said, most agree that, regardless of its faults, our democratic system of government is the best in the world. William Howard Taft stated, "We are imperfect. We cannot expect a perfect government." I concur. We will never reach perfection, but there are some possible changes that would certainly give the public more confidence in the political process.

First, it is time to reform campaign finance practices. Those running for political office today must be bankrolled to the tune of millions of dollars to even consider political office, even on the state level. Does this spending deter otherwise qualified candidates from pursuing office? Is politics a "rich" person's game? Would an Abe Lincoln, who tried to personally finance his 1858 Senate race, be able to compete today since the contest left him bankrupt?

Campaign spending reached an all-time high in the last presidential race. For the first time, according to Federal Election

Commission statistics, the candidates spent over $1 billion during the 2008 election. The exact amount, $1.7 billion, more than doubled the amount spent four years before. Barak Obama outspent John McCain by a margin of 4 to 1. McCain accepted $84.1 million that public finance funds offered him for the campaign, which barred him from receiving any private donations. Obama, however, was the first candidate ever to reject federal funding for the general election. This allowed him to raise and spend a whopping $740.6 million.

A few states have initiated a program called "Clean Money, Clean Elections." This method of control sounds promising. It gives every candidate a set amount of money. The candidates qualify for the funds by collecting a specific number of signatures and small contributions. If they receive this public funding, they are not allowed to accept outside donations or to use their own personal money. Candidates can receive matching funds up to a limit if they are outspent by candidates who are privately funded, or if they are attacked in the media by independent organizations. For example, if a candidate is supported by a labor union and receives funds from them, the opposing candidate may qualify for matching funds. In the 2012 election, Super Pacs played a significant role in media control. Although they have no ties to a candidate, donors can give large sums of money to a Super Pac with no limit, who buy advertising on all TV stations throughout the United States. Although legal, to me, this is just a way to side step the regulations on campaign funding.

This is the basic difference between a system many say is *broken;* currently, no extra funds are available for candidates who do not receive independent support from union or other corporate organizations. Supporters claim that Clean Elections matching funds have been highly effective at leveling the playing field in states implementing the system, such as Arizona and Maine.

In fact, a clause in the Bipartisan Campaign Reform Act of 2002, often referred to as the McCain-Feingold Act, required the non-partisan General Accounting Office to conduct a study of Clean

Elections programs in the states using the system. A recent study by the Center for Governmental Studies found that Clean Elections programs resulted in more candidates, more competition, more voter participation, and less influence-peddling.

The debate continues, however, with the latest court ruling stating that to limit campaign funding by unions and corporations violated these organizations' First Amendment rights (Citizens United v. Federal Election Commission, Jan, 2010). Basically, unions and corporations are not to be barred from promoting the election of one candidate over another. I'm sure there will be more attempts to somehow finance races more evenly, as campaign finance reform is a hot topic for both Republicans and Democrats.

Limits on Mud-slinging

The attempts to curb negative campaigning resulted in adding a rule to the McCain-Feingold Act that required every candidate for federal office to identify the source of his or her funding. Also, in national elections—from Congress up to the office of the president—television ads must feature the candidate, identifying himself or herself by name and stating, "I have approved this message." I'm sure you have seen those ads.

The general belief was that if the person, or candidate, had to personally claim responsibility for the content of the ad, perhaps there would be less mud-slinging and negative rhetoric. Unfortunately, there has actually been no noticeable effect on the tone of campaigns.

Media intrusion into the private lives of candidates will most likely continue, too. It is up to us, the voters, to determine when such reporting oversteps the public's need to know and borders on defamation of character or libel. In my opinion, we do need to know if a candidate has a criminal record, a fraudulent past, or has had moral issues. Like professional athletes, political office seekers should be role models. The president of the United States certainly should be a role model to all countrymen. However, some attacks from both political parties are downright brutal for the candidate and their family. My hope would be for an appointed panel or board to approve personal campaign attacks before airing. The information could be examined for credibility and relevancy before allowing reputations to be destroyed or a candidate's family to be permanently hurt.

Along these same lines, I am not sure that ministers, priests, or denominational leaders should be heavily involved in endorsing candidates. It has always been my opinion that the minister's first calling is to fulfill the command of the New Testament to preach the Gospel and the salvation of souls. I know some might disagree, but for me, when I hear of a minister instructing his congregation or followers as to how they should vote, I remember how ardently our forefathers supported the separation of church and state. There may be exceptions, such as Reverend Martin Luther King. However, Dr. King was heading up a cause much greater than endorsing a candidate; he wanted others to catch his dream of eradicating racism in America.

Choosing a President

I was asked recently what qualities to look for in a person I would support for president. I suppose the most important characteristic to me is the person's ability to communicate. A candidate could be the most patriotic, sincere, intelligent, wise, and experienced candidate, but if he/she can't articulate well, everything else is for naught. A man I was privileged to know and work with on several occasions was President Ronald Reagan, who is called "The Great Communicator." When he spoke, he exuded confidence, security and steady calm. He made us feel safe, strong, and unified. Reagan's sense of humor was evident when he spoke, and he was not afraid to let the public see his caring heart as well.

I marvel how George Washington, who tried to decline the presidency on several occasions, pulled our ragtag colonies together to form a new nation that won our independence and gained the admiration of the world. I admire President Eisenhower and

President George Herbert Walker Bush as military heroes, and believe President Kennedy was a brilliant young president who was tragically cut down in his prime. Reagan, however, was the complete package.

With all the domestic issues on the line, and the foreign policy decisions the president must make daily, we realize more than ever that it is our duty to study the candidates, know the issues, and pray for wisdom as we elect leaders. No matter who the eventual winner of the election happens to be, there is one more duty....

Pray for the President

The Bible clearly directs us to pray for those in authority, those in leadership over us. If we truly believe prayer works, then we will believe that God can and will speak to the heart of a president who makes decisions for us all. God can give him guidance, direction, and put men and women in place who will offer wisdom and godly counsel. We need to pray for our president, whether you voted for him or not. Regardless of party affiliation, we need to pray that our president will remain physically sound, healthy, protected from illness, injury, or attack. We also need to pray for the president's family.

As Kim and I and our boys pray for our leaders, we realize the truth of the old saying by E. M. Bounds: "Preaching moves men, but prayer moves God." We rely on God to intervene on our nation's behalf in all issues that concern us at home and abroad. (The 30-Day Devotional in the back of this book will give you direction as you join us to pray for all national, state, and city leaders.) As assuredly as it is our duty as citizens to vote, it is our duty as Christians to pray.

Why Should You Vote?

- Because voting is your duty as a citizen.
- Your vote does count.
- Voting is the only way to preserve our freedom.

- Voting is a privilege not to be taken lightly and sets an example for others.

Not too long ago, Frank Buckles, the last surviving veteran of World War I, died at 100 years of age. In 1917 the sixteen-year-old Buckles lied about his age in order to enlist in the Army. During World War I, he was stationed in England and France; during World War II, he was in a Japanese prison camp for three years. The old gentleman was sharp to the end, serving as an honorary chairman for the World War I Memorial Foundation. His funeral was befitting a hero. The army's oldest active duty regiment, the 3rd Infantry, handled the honors. Army Corporal Frank Buckles was buried at Arlington, and President Obama and his wife visited his grave to pay their respects.

I meet them all the time, all ages, from all over our great country. They are the veterans, like Frank Buckles, who were willing to die to protect our rights, even the right to speak against our own government. Next time you show up at the polls and slap that "I Voted" sticker on your shirt, remember Frank Buckles and the thousands upon thousands of other men and women who made it possible.

Thanks for "God Bless the U.S. A."

Dear Mr. Greenwood,

My name is Mark Ziperski and I live with my family in New Auburn, Wisconsin. My 3rd and last son has just graduated from high school in New Auburn. He has received a scholarship called "Let us Never Forget." It is a non-profit organization started in Cincinnati. They choose to honor one family per state that lost a military member in the line of duty. This year they picked Pauline Knutson, a single mother of two daughters who serve in the armed forces. One of her daughters, 2nd Lt. Tracy Alger, was deployed in 2007 to Iraq. She graduated from the University of River Falls in graphic design but was troubled by the need for soldiers in Iraq. She chose to serve her country because of her devotion to help others.

Tracy died in April, 2007 when an IUD was detonated, killing her and the driver of the truck they were in. I only mention this because Tracy was on the flight to Iraq when apparently you met her and had a conversation with her on this flight. I thought you would like to know that God had chosen that day for you to meet her. I think of this occasionally and remember what she told her mother about meeting you. It brings tears to my eyes when occasionally I dwell on this too long, especially when I'm listening to you sing "God Bless the U.S.A."

I know her mother thinks about her every day and would greatly appreciate a letter of encouragement or a phone call from you. Thank you sincerely and mercifully for all you do.

—In His service until that time,

Mark Ziperski

New Auburn, Wisconsin

A Nation of Givers

We make a living by what we get, but we make a life by what we give.

—Winston Churchill

Patriotism, gratitude, and generosity define our American way of life.

—Lee Greenwood

Some childhood memories of life on my grandparents' farm remain vivid after all these years. I still recall the blossoms exploding like huge pink and white fluffy snowballs on the almond trees. The midnight jasmine that crawled up from the ground to cover the top of the trailer where we lived was strong and sweet. I close my eyes and see the cherry trees, the peach trees, the grapevines that grew up and over the dove cage next to the house. On a hot summer day, I would grab a bunch of grapes hanging overhead from the arbor and sit on the ground with my back against the house, eating my fill. We also grew artichokes, crab apples, and vegetables of all kinds. We had three cows and about a thousand chickens we raised each year. At fourteen, I knew how to wring a chicken's neck, pluck it, and prepare it for dinner. We were not wealthy, but we certainly never went hungry, because we raised our own food.

My grandparents made a decent living from sharecropping. They never actually owned land themselves, but farmed the land for the owner and stored the crops in his barns. We received a portion of the proceeds from selling produce and lived off the rest. It was common for my grandfather to barter for other goods the family needed. I recall how he would trade produce for tractor parts, even clothing and other essentials. My grandparents made sure my basic needs were met, but if I wanted anything extra, I had to work for it. I can remember picking sweet peas, putting them in small bouquets, and then heading down to Mr. Si's Chinese Market to sell them. The money made was mine to keep, so, I paid for my own clothes or any extra things I wanted.

I remember how neighbors would come together to help each other. Whether it was sharing food, harvesting a crop, helping with a building project, or caring for the sick, neighbors could be relied on in times of need. As if on cue, several people would show up to help us string beans or husk corn. They would sit on the back porch or at the kitchen table and visit while they worked for hours. That's just what neighbors did. Even as a child I understood how important it was to help others when they needed help. Our neighbors and friends didn't want recognition and they didn't want anything in return. These were just really good people who taught me how to give just for the sake of giving.

—Lee

By the time I reached eleven years of age, farming was being phased out due to grain subsidizing to Russia. The U. S. government was paying farmers not to farm, to manage the glut in the market. So when farming became unprofitable, my grandparents built small cottages on the property and rented them out. This is how they made their living for the rest of their lives. My grandparents would never be rich, but needs were met and they passed down to me a work ethic I value everyday.

My memories of elementary school are still vivid. There were no gangs yet, but the rich kids formed clubs and cliques. As a farmer, I was considered lower than middle class. I was literally from the other side of the tracks. The railroad ran right behind our farmhouse and separated us from the subdivision that surrounded the high school I would later attend. It bothered me not to be accepted by the more popular boys. Each day I was given twenty-five cents for lunch and I would give that to one of the boys to allow me to hang with the group during recess. I was never part of the "in" crowd in school, but by the time I was a junior in high school, my musical talents were being noticed and even appreciated by my classmates. I never had to worry about being accepted ever again.

Just when I thought I would get a little respect as a freshman at the junior high school level, we moved from Sacramento to Anaheim, where the high school there included the ninth grade. I mentioned in Chapter Six how we lived near Disneyland. So, I found myself back at the bottom of the pecking order, and wouldn't you know? When I moved back a year later to attend high school in Sacramento, which was a three year high school, I was still at the bottom as a sophomore. I just couldn't win. However, by that time, I was a working musician playing several nights during the week just like my mother had in the 1940s. I was making money and no longer paid attention to the cliques.

I hold no bitterness or regret over the self-imposed alienation I knew as a kid. I had different dreams, a different focus. I would be on my own, working in Vegas before I turned seventeen.

My grandparents were my mentors as well as my guardians, and I learned so much from both of them. I didn't have a big brother or any other positive male influence in my life, but we did have a neighbor named Margie who looked after me. I took tap dance lessons from her and she became a friend, one in whom I could confide. Other than Margie and my sister Patricia, I really can't think of anyone else who helped me through those difficult years. It was clear early on that I needed to develop a personal inner strength, a belief in myself and my dreams, because no one else was going to pave the way.

In Vegas, I chiseled out a living based on my talent and needs. For many years I managed to survive; at one point becoming a card dealer at a casino to augment my income. Then, in 1974, I heard a song on the radio which I loved instantly. The song was "Please Come to Boston" by Dave Loggins. I found the album that included the song and saw that it was produced by Jerry Crutchfield, head of MCA Music at the time. I took a chance and contacted Jerry in Nashville. In that conversation, I was bold enough to ask him to come to Vegas to hear me perform. Since he would be making a trip soon to L.A., he said he'd be happy to stop over in Nevada to hear me sing. I was pretty excited. Jerry met me at The Flamingo where I was working in the lounge with Bill Medley; Elvis was in the main room. After my set, we talked for a few minutes, and Jerry agreed to pitch me to the MCA label. Things happened pretty fast after that. I went to Los Angeles for a demo session at MCA music. We cut four sides with some studio players from LA and Jerry took them to Nashville for review with the head of the label, Jim Fogelsong. It wasn't long after that, I was signed as an artist at MCA records.

As mentioned, my first lessons on giving were taught by caring neighbors and friends. I made an early commitment that if I were ever successful and financially capable, I would help others who needed a handup, not a handout. Many Americans want to help others, especially those who can't help themselves. Is there something distinctive about America that makes us a nation of givers? Why do we care so deeply about the needs of others?

Kim and I recently were in Phoenix, Arizona, for Muhammed Ali's Fight Night event. One of the honorees of the evening was Red McCombs. Red is the former owner of the San Antonio Spurs and a couple of other NBA franchises. He is also the founder of Red McCombs Automotive Group and co-founder of Clear Channel Communications. The McCombs School of Business at the

University of Texas is named in his honor, and he was recognized by *Forbes* magazine as one of the top 400 richest Americans of 2005. In accepting his award for the evening, Red made the following comment: "There is more philanthropy in the United States than the rest of the world combined."

Why Do We Care?

According to statistics, in 2005 Americans contributed $212 billion to various philanthropic causes. Other countries with similar needs have nowhere near our level of commitment to giving, but our society would be seriously affected without this kind of contribution to the welfare of our citizens.

Some would say our nation's Christian roots compel us to be charitable. The Bible instructs us to give in the name of the Lord (see Ephesians 3:17). The book of Acts cites many examples of how the early church was dedicated to meeting the needs of orphans, widows, and the poor. Certainly, people of faith are going to be more aware of the needs of others and more willing to help.

This idea was confirmed by Syracuse professor Arthur Brooks who studied charitable giving in the United States and discovered that "religious conservatives" give more than any other identifiable group. In his book *Who Really Cares?*, Brooks concludes that this segment of our population gives 30 percent more to charity than those who describe themselves as "liberals," despite the fact that liberals have higher average incomes than conservatives. "Religious people," Brooks says, "are more charitable in every measurable nonreligious way." I am sure it is because people of faith feel accountable to God to bless others when capable of doing so.

Brooks also found that conservatives donate more in time, services, and even blood than other Americans. He went so far as to estimate that if liberals and moderates gave as much blood as conservatives do, the blood supply would increase by about 45 percent. So, on average, a person who attends church and is "conservative" will give one hundred times more—and fifty times more to secular charities—than a person who does not attend religious services and is a self-described "liberal." This is only one person's opinion and I don't necessarily agree.

Those findings aside, I believe there is yet another deeply rooted reason as to why we care. Caring is part of our inbred heritage. In the Mayflower Compact of 1620, the Pilgrims, while still offshore but in American waters, declared that they "solemnly and mutually, in the Presence of God and one another, combine ourselves together into a civil Body Politick, for our better Ordering and Preservation." The Pilgrims knew that if they were to survive the untamed new world, they would need to "combine themselves together." Thus, when the early colonies were settled, they were made up of people who became socially responsible for the public good. This is why settlements such as Pennsylvania, Virginia, and Massachusetts were often referred to as "commonwealths," which meant all members contributed to the "common wealth." This collaboration was the forerunner of the first established American government.

I cannot imagine the hardships encountered by these dauntless men and women as they charted a never-before-traveled course to settle this land. They had no way of knowing they were laying the foundation for the greatest nation the world has ever known. Yet there seemed to be an innate understanding of sharing, volunteering, helping one another, and being responsible for and to each other—all for the betterment of a new society.

One of our most influential forefathers laid the foundation for philanthropy in the early days of the new republic. Benjamin Franklin is referred to as "the first great American" partly because he oriented his life around helping to meet the needs of others. As a young businessman in 1727, he formed a twelve-member club, called the "Junto," that met every Friday evening to discuss current events and issues. One of the four qualifications for membership was a "love of mankind in general." The Junto became a vehicle to discuss philanthropic ideas, to raise public awareness, to recruit volunteers when needed, and to raise funds. In 1729 Franklin founded the *Philadelphia Gazette* and the public became more aware of ongoing needs within the communities. It was Franklin who first instigated the creation of volunteer fire associations, hospitals, educational institutions, and public libraries. He also convinced colonists of the need for paving and patrolling public streets. He encouraged the establishment of town hall meeting places, knowing it would be necessary to give citizens a voice in an independent society.

Years later it was Franklin, among others, who urged farmers and tradesmen to volunteer in the War of Independence. The farmers formed voluntary associations referred to as "Minutemen," men who were ready to leave their farms and take up arms against the British at a moment's notice. Another example is Paul Revere, who organized volunteers to observe the movement of British troops, then rode on horseback to rally the towns around Boston.

The first army, the Continental Army of the United States, was composed of volunteers, financed by donations. George Washington was Commanding General of the army and served for many years without pay "for the public good." Political associations, like the famous Sons of Liberty, sprang up in every city, flaming the desire for independence.

Even the signers of The Declaration of Independence acted as a philanthropy-driven group when creating this voluntary pledge, a mission statement to each other:

> We the people of the United States, in order to form a more perfect union, establish justice, insure domestic tranquility, provide for the common defence, promote the general welfare, and secure the blessings of liberty to ourselves and our posterity, do ordain and establish this Constitution for the United States of America.

Alexander Hamilton noted that in creating a new nation, Americans were acting for the benefit of all mankind: "This adds the inducements of philanthropy to those of patriotism." In his plea for independence, "Common Sense," Thomas Paine wrote: "The cause of America in a great measure is the cause of all mankind."

Giving wasn't just about the rich helping the poor. Philanthropy focused on quality of life for all citizens. The United States was not only created by philanthropy, but we became a nation dedicated to giving to others. Early founders saw even our nation's existence as a gift to humanity.

When the American Revolution began, Concord, Massachusetts had become a center for philanthropy and volunteerism. It is fitting then that Ralph Waldo Emerson should write these immortal words in the "Concord Hymn": "Here once the embattled farmers stood, and fired the shot heard 'round the world."

These brave countrymen stood their ground at Concord, pledging their lives to independence. These were the men and women who first developed our American culture and character, including the desire to benefit others in need.

In the 1830s, when Frenchman Alexis de Tocqueville came to study American life, he noted the country's giving spirit with some surprise. In his two-volume work, *Democracy in America,* he observed that Americans did not rely on the government, the aristocracy, or the church to solve their problems. They did it themselves through voluntary philanthropic associations, or "private initiatives for public good, focusing on quality of life." He found that this characteristic permeated American life and culture and was the key to America's democratic society.

Even the horror of the nation's Civil War saw both sides involved in volunteerism and giving. Armies of volunteers, in both the North and the South, sold bonds and stockpiled contributions, praying for quick resolution. Following the war, the rebuilding of the South was, in itself, a testament to the nation's caring spirit.

Later, at the turn of the century, Andrew Carnegie and well-to-do families like the Rockefellers would encourage the rich to leave their wealth not only to their own families, but to take care of public needs and interests as well. Through the Great Depression, two world wars, and even during our present-day struggles with the economy, the long history of philanthropy is so deeply entrenched into our psyche that it is part of our way of life. Giving generously is commonplace and infused into our DNA. There are now more than 965,000 charitable tax-exempt organizations, employing millions, supported by the gifts of individuals and private foundations and bolstered by armies of volunteers.

The founding fathers could never have dreamed or imagined that one day American citizens would give to various causes to the tune of millions of dollars every year. We care today for many reasons, but first, because the earliest Americans taught us to care.

Are Children Catching the Spirit of Giving?

We have so much in our country—more material wealth than any other generation—but I hope we are not creating a society where the act of acquiring is more important than the act of giving. "Keeping up with the Joneses" or one-upping the neighbor is all too important to some. Selfishness is one of those traits that parents must attempt to correct, or we risk creating adults who feel entitled to everything without earning it or appreciating it. Perhaps you've heard the saying, "Kids today know the price of everything, but the value of nothing." It is up to parents to teach children the value of work, to instill gratefulness, sharing, and awareness of the needs of others. As our own sons grow and mature, I see them developing a greater interest and willingness to help others.

Children learn best by example, so Kim and I make sure our boys know about the charities we support. We tithe and give to mission projects sponsored by our church, but we give to other causes, too. We are involved in HopeHouse International, partially in response to our ties with its founder, our friend, Deneen Turner. Deneen's mother escaped from Ukraine during World War II, and Deneen introduced us to this wonderful organization a few years ago. HopeHouse International exists so that orphans can be adopted by helping Ukrainian Christian couples acquire adequate housing, which makes them eligible (according to their government) to adopt three or more children. Mrs. Turner's Ukranian heritage and personal background has given her a passion for orphaned children. She and her family have been actively involved in helping orphans, remaining steadfast and committed to this mission for over twenty years. (For more information see the Web site for HopeHouse International: www.hopehouseinternational.org.)

Another organization we support is Operation Never Forgotten, a wonderful, non-profit group dedicated to supporting deployed troops, wounded warriors, fallen heroes, and our military families. ONF creates public service announcements connecting the military and civilian communities. They also place signs in airports, food stores and malls, broadcast television and radio spots, and sponsor a nationwide billboard campaign in support of our military. One special ONF event each year is a benefit called Operation SAS (Sports, Afield and Stream). Wounded Warriors are invited to experience a great time of sporting, hunting, and fishing in Montana. This year, sixty-five soldiers and their families participated and were introduced to winter sports. For many, this is a time of restoration and healing. I was privileged to be named a spokesperson for ONF who do so much to show appreciation to our military men and women and their families. (Check out their Web site at: www.operationneverforgotten.org.) We are also heavily involved with Products for Good, a group that raises money through the sale of unique liberated Iraqi coins, acquired during the Gulf War. This organization gives thousand of dollars to our wounded warriors through many charities including the U.S.O. I am again privileged to serve as spokesperson for this great company. (See the Web site at: www.productsforgood.com).

Kim and I enjoy looking for ways in which we can help others in need. Many opportunities appear randomly, and we consider each a nudge from God. For example, we have discovered the Boys and Girls Clubs of America, who yearly provide mentorship for hundreds of children, including at-risk kids who need direction and love. I, along with other country and gospel artists, am also privileged to be part of Sean Hannity's Freedom Alliance Concerts. The organization benefitting from the concerts is the Freedom Alliance Scholarship Fund, a charity actually established by Oliver North to help children of fallen soldiers continue their education. In its eighth year, the Freedom Alliance Concerts have raised over $10 million for the fund.

Finally, I serve proudly on the advisory board of The Challenger Commission, an organization established following the Challenger shuttle disaster. The founder, June Scobee Rogers, widow of Challenger crew chief Dick Scobee, keeps the memory of the shuttle's crew alive by serving the youth of America with educational facilities erected around the United States, now including North America. They invite children of all ages, and adults, to be part of a mission in space. They challenge all of us to think and dream about the future of America and the entire human race. For a complete history and to view Challenger centers, log on to www.challenger.org.

As for my wife and me, we want our children to see for themselves the deplorable living conditions of children in so many other parts of the world and how blessed they are to live in America. It is important that they see the needs all around them and respond to those needs. Ruth Stafford Peale, the wife of Reverend Norman Vincent Peale who wrote *The Power of Positive Thinking*, lived by a motto that I hope our sons and all young people embrace: "Find a need and fill it." What a wonderful way to live—looking for needs we can meet. Living out that motto brings purpose, direction, and real satisfaction to anyone's life, young and old alike.

To Whom Do we Give?

As the welfare debate rages, the fact remains that Americans are generous to the core and, no matter the party affiliation, most want to meet the needs of those who cannot help themselves. This desire shows up in men like actor, Paul Newman, who created an entire food company so that children could benefit from the proceeds. By the time of Newman's death in 2008, the company had donated over $300 million to thousands of charities. How about the gift that Warren Buffett made to the Bill and Linda Gates Foundation, to help underprivileged countries? The $31 billion gift is the largest ever single donation.

It was the generosity of Americans that funded causes such as anti-slavery, women's suffrage, civil rights, environmental conservation, war efforts, and the reconstruction of cities and nations. American philanthropy established and maintains educational systems, schools and universities nation-wide. It is the major source of income for fine arts and performing arts, religious or faith-based programs, humanitarian causes, and animal rights and care. Americans have taken it upon themselves to meet challenges and provide opportunities that government or business wouldn't or couldn't address by donating millions to charities world-wide.

One of my great concerns is that the generations to come will not embrace the lifestyle of caring, that America is known for. This is why we must work hard to educate our children about the importance of generosity, stewardship, social responsibility, and even sacrificial giving. Giving is an acquired skill that is taught, then nurtured over time. It is truly "more blessed to give, than to receive." There are more ways to give, than just giving money. I thank God for the people who gave their time, energy, concern, council, and most of all their love to me. Those things that cannot be measured by a dollar amount are the most valuable.

On a personal level, we should take the time to thank those who invested in our lives, who believed in us when no one else gave us a thought, who said that thing that inspired us, shared that story or listened to our dreams. Sure, we Americans pride ourselves on working hard and pulling ourselves up "by our own boot-straps", but usually in the background of our successes are parents, teachers, friends, and, or a spouse to whom we owe so much. Thank them today.

A blurb I wrote for the Operation Never Forgotten Web site sums up my feelings for this important topic: "Patriotism, gratitude and generosity define our American way of life." May it always be so.

Thanks for "God Bless the U.S. A."

Dear Lee,

Thank you very much for your kind reply. The ceremony was all so extremely moving. Steve and Trisha landed at Lunken Airport in Cincinnati in a small jet with their son, Pfc Seth Blevin's casket. Lunken is the smaller private airport and is probably fifty miles from where the funeral and burial were to take place. There was a large motorcade accompanying the hearse.

From Georgetown on into Sardinia the ENTIRE WAY was lined with yellow ribbons every fifty feet or so!! The local life squads, fire departments, and American Legion organized and placed the ribbons. As the motorcade made its way through the small towns along the way, the road was packed with those paying respects and fire trucks were parked at various locations flying the colors on the extended ladders. Seth's casket was presented at the high school where he graduated for a few hours on the day before the funeral.

Literally thousands of people waited hours to pay respects and to extend condolences to Steve and his family. I have no idea how they were able to hold up like they did. They were on their feet for over six hours shaking hands and receiving hugs from friends, and people they didn't even know. Steve was quoted in the paper that as he rode in the motorcade, one of the things that made the biggest impression on him was the fact that he saw people crying who he knew had never met Seth. While it was an event that brought the community together, I can only pray that it is something that we never have to go through again. Your song does much to encourage and comfort those who mourn the passing of these wonderful young soldiers. Thank you so very much for your kindness. It is with the fervent hope that next time we speak it will be for something more joyful.

—Sincerely and with best regards,
Mike Pasquale
June, 2011

Where Are The Heroes?

Those who say we're in a time when there are no heroes, they just don't know where to look.

—Ronald Reagan

As you get older, it is harder to have heroes, but it is sort of necessary.

—Ernest Hemingway

Hard times don't create heroes. It is during the hard times when the hero within us is revealed.

—Bob Riley

I grew up thinking Roy Rogers was the quintessential hero. I could hardly wait for each Saturday morning episode of *The Roy Rogers Show* on television. The "King of the Cowboys," spoke kindly, tipped his hat to ladies, loved Dale Evans and his horse, Trigger, and sang and played the guitar. I even loved Roy's sidekick, Pat Brady, and Pat's jeep, Nellybelle. The show aired from 1951 to 1957, when Roy and Dale began their television variety show.

Many may recall that Roy never shot a bad guy. Instead, he would shoot the gun out of the villain's hand or win in a fist fight to take him in alive. Each show ended with Dale and Roy singing "Happy Trails to You."

I had real-life heroes, too, like baseball's Babe Ruth and Joe DiMaggio. Later, as I developed a love for music, there were musicians and singers I admired. About the time I started playing the sax, I came to enjoy the music of Stan Kenton, Count Basie, the Dorsey brothers, Earl Bostic and Sam Butera. The singers included Roy Rogers and the Sons of the Pioneers, Sam Cooke, Bobby Darin, Ronnie Milsap, Kenny Rogers and Elton John.

Of course, Elvis came along in the '50s, establishing that rock 'n roll was here to stay. Later the Beatles made their mark on music history. Even before moving to Nevada in 1961, I was aware of country music, particularly the Grand Old Opry from Nashville, Tennessee. But when I heard the recording of Ray Charles's album entitled "C & W," I became an instant fan. The success of this album demonstrated to me that talented people can cross genres and make great music. With the marriage of rhythm and blues, jazz, and country, I found my own style.

These great artists were heroes to me in the sense that I wanted to learn from all of them. However, at this point in my life, the meaning of the word hero has evolved into something that means much more. We have always had them, but now, as never before, America needs men and women who are authentic. We need a hero!

—Lee

On January 28, 1986, millions of Americans, including schoolchildren, saw the Challenger lift off from the Kennedy Space Center, then watched in horror seventy-four seconds later as the shuttle capsule exploded on live television. Gone were the seven brave crew members, including Christa McAuliffe, a teacher from New Hampshire.

Hours later, President Reagan addressed a shocked nation: "The crew of the space shuttle, Challenger, honored us by the manner in which they lived their lives. We will never forget them, nor the last time we saw them this morning, as they prepared for the journey and waved goodbye and 'slipped the surly bonds of earth' to 'touch the face of God.'"

The words Reagan quoted from poet John Magee, in his poem entitled "High Flight," hang in the air even now:

Oh, I have slipped the surly bonds of earth,
And danced the skies on laughter-silvered wings;
Sunward I've climbed, and joined the tumbling mirth
Of sun-split clouds,—and done a hundred things
You have not dreamed of... wheeled and soared and swung
High in the sunlit silence. Hov'ring there
I've chased the shouting wind along, and flung
My eager craft through footless halls of air....
Up, up the long, delirious, burning blue
I've topped the wind-swept heights with easy grace
Where never lark or even eagle flew.
And, while with silent lifting mind I've trod
The high untrespassed sanctity of space,
Put out my hand and touched the face of God.

I consider the crew of the Challenger among some of our country's greatest heroes. One of them was NASA astronaut and commander of the Challenger, Dick Scobee. June Scobee, Dick's widow, later married Army Lieutenant General Don Rodgers, now retired. Don had also lived through the tragedy of losing his first wife years earlier to a serious illness. Kim and I are honored to know June and Don. They, in fact, are godparents to our sons.

Michael Bolton recorded a song titled "Go the Distance," from the animated motion picture, *Hercules*, which I often perform because I love its message. One line in the song especially resonates: "A hero's strength is measured by his heart." It's that something that makes heroes of us all at certain times. When our back is against the wall, when the bills mount up, when relationships are difficult, when our dreams have fallen through, life's heroes keep going, keep trying, even when it looks like failure is imminent.

Why? What is it that makes some crumble at the sight of the huge daunting mountain, while other stalwart souls can hardly wait for the climb? Where are the heroes of today? Who are the men and women we can point to and say to our children, "Be like that?"

Suppose you could go back in history and talk to anyone you chose about some decision you need to make in your life right now. Who would you visit with, and why? Would it be Moses, Abraham Lincoln, Mother Teresa. Alexander the Great, or Jesus? Maybe it would be someone from your own family who has passed away—a grandfather, a brother, a spouse.

As strange as it may sound, heroes who have gone before *are* speaking to us. Their voices aren't bombastic and preachy, but more like whispers as they lean in to tell us their stories. If we listen closely, we will learn what it took for them to make the decisions that changed the shape of a nation, a battle, an enterprise, and human lives. This is what heroes do—they show us the way.

When I was a young man, working hard on my grandparents' farm, I listened to my grandfather when he told me how to maneuver a tractor through muddy ground, repair a fence, or care for a sick animal. When my grandfather said, "Lee, let me help you. Here's what you do," I never said, "No, I don't want you to show me!" You see, I knew he had done the task many times before and he would show me how to do it the right way. Heroes do the same. They show us the right way, the best way.

American heroes have come from all walks of life, from different economic and educational backgrounds; every generation boasts a few. One thing about America is that we are not easily given to hero worship. Author Michael Korda, in his book, *Ike: An American Hero,* explains that our democratic view makes us leery of singling out one person as elite because we value equality so much. He cites other examples such as France, which claims a national passion for Napoleon Bonaparte. England refers to Winston Churchill in heroic terms. Russia's Peter the Great is their most recognizable and enduring hero. America has produced many great men and women who accomplished remarkable things since the birth of our nation, but when you think about it, there is not one person who stands out above the rest.

Korda speculates one reason for this is our desire to know everything about everyone. We dig through a person's past to discover their mistakes, their weaknesses, their flaws. Add to that an aggressive media, which report every impropriety, large or small, and Americans are quick to point out that no one is perfect.

That is not to say, however, that heroes don't live among us. We can point to many in our historical past. While writing this chapter, I thought of so many men and women, past and present, whom I would consider heroic. It would be impossible to include all of their stories in one chapter. There are, however, certain characteristics we can attribute to those whom we call heroes.

Heroes "Go Beyond Survival"

Heroes accomplish extraordinary exploits when called upon in moments of extreme duress or danger. When U.S. Navy Captain Gerald Coffee guides his RA-5C reconnaissance jet over North Vietnam in February of 1966, he knew the risk he was taking. He had escaped serious situations before, but as the jet suddenly came under fire and he prepared to eject, he knew this was the most serious of all. Immediately captured on the ground, Capt. Coffee was taken to the notorious "Hanoi Hilton" prison, where he would endure the next seven years of routine torture and solitary confinement.

In a remarkable account of those seven long years, Capt. Coffee speaks of the day he refused to become a broken man. Instead, he determined that for as long as the ordeal lasted, he would use the time to learn, to become a better man, to live to tell others that faith, honor, and the human spirit can triumph, even in the direst of circumstances. In his book *Beyond Survival,* Coffee recounts the elements that helped him not just survive but to go "beyond survival."

Communication kept the prisoners connected even though verbal communication was not allowed. Through a clever new language invented by the prisoners, the alphabet was used and a "tap code" utilized to relay information and messages back and forth. *Leadership* was redefined and consisted not only of believing in his senior officers, but a determined effort to maintain personal accountability and integrity. *Mastering change* was critical when all the strength he could count on was the strength within himself. Teamwork was the backdrop for the prisoners' motto: "Unity Over Self." Not even the North Vietnamese could break such strong and stalwart loyalty to each other. *Humor* would be a necessary ally to alleviate the cramped, filthy conditions and cruel treatment.

Overcoming adversity became the focused goal everyday. He writes of walking several miles a day in a tiny cell. Three steps and a turn back and forth again and again, because his mission was to return home better, tougher, stronger.

Then one day in 1973, it was over. One of the longest-held prisoners of the Vietnam War, Capt. Gerald Coffee returned to his family and to his country with honor intact. Such heroes inspire us to face our own day-to-day challenges with a new attitude, a new determination. Today Capt. Coffee is a sought-after speaker who shares his experiences and motivates others to "go beyond" survival. Kim and I were privileged to meet and hear Capt. Coffee recently and were moved to tears as he explained a table set for honoring Prisoners of War and the Missing in Action. It was riveting.

The small table was set for one, symbolizing one prisoner against his oppressors. The tablecloth was white, symbolizing the purity of these men to respond to their country's call. A single rose in a vase represented the family and loved ones awaiting his return. A red ribbon tied to the vase was the same worn by thousands who demand a proper accounting for our missing. The bread plate held a slice of lemon, a reminder of their bitter fate. Also, there was salt on the bread plate, symbolic of a family's tears as they wait and hope. The glass on the table was inverted because those missing could not raise the glass to toast with us. And the chair at the table was empty...enough said.

As Capt. Coffee closed the presentation, he raised his glass and said, "Remember, all of you who served with them and called them comrades, who depended on their might and aid and relied on them... for surely...they have not forsaken you. And then a toast to those soldiers all over the world." It was a moment we will never forget.

Heroes are like Captain Gerald Coffey; ready when called upon, drawing on everything they have learned, felt, and believed for that single moment when it is all on the line.

In 1982 I received an MIA bracelet in honor of Captain John W. Consolvo, Jr., an F-4 Pilot for the Marines who was shot down over South Vietnam on May 7, 1972. I made a personal commitment to wear it for the rest of my life or until Captain Consolvo was accounted for. I learned Captain Consolvo was from Virginia and that his father was a World War II veteran of the Battle of the Bulge. When I look at the bracelet I've worn for so many years, I feel connected to a family that prays for some word regarding the whereabouts of their American hero. Captain Coffey's words only deepened my determination to honor his memory for as long as it takes to bring him home.

Heroes Seize the Moment

Heroes respond to crisis as if they have been preparing all their lives for that moment. US Airways Captain Chesley Sullenberger comes to mind. In 2009, "Sully," as he was affectionately called, was piloting Flight #1549 when a flock of birds disabled both of the plane's engines ninety seconds after takeoff from New York's LaGuardia Airport. With 155 passengers on board, Sullenberger weighed every option and determined that the best chance for survival was to set the plane down in the Hudson River, just off Manhattan. He said it was "the worst sickening, pit-of-your-stomach, falling-through-the-floor feeling" that he had ever experienced.

Sullenberger remained calm and collected as he expertly glided the plane onto the surface of the water. All lives were saved. Later recounting the experience to the media, he said, "One way of looking at this might be that for 42 years, I've been making small, regular deposits in this bank of experience, education, and training. And on January 15, 2009, the balance was sufficient so that I could make a very large withdrawal." Heroes seize the moment when all they have been trained to do may determine the safety and destiny of others.

Heroes Have Changed America

We benefit from many Americans who have impacted or changed our lives for the better. Inventors like Thomas Edison and Henry Ford; pioneers of flight like the Wright brothers, Amelia Earhart, Charles Lindbergh, and John Glenn; environmentalists like John Muir; authors like Carl Sandberg, Robert Frost, Mark Twain; businessmen who plotted the first railroads and built the first cities. We owe so much to such brilliant men and women. But there are others whose influence has changed the way we think, react, and feel toward each other.

If you take I-40 east from Nashville, go about 140 miles to the Oak Ridge Turnpike, than travel north a bit, you will come to Clinton, Tennessee. Clinton is a town that once was home to twelve young people who became unlikely heroes at a time when our nation needed them most. They are referred to as the "Clinton 12"—twelve African-American students who were the first to integrate an all-white school in 1956.

A great documentary film, *The Clinton 12,* was recently produced. telling their story. The film included interviews with former teachers, citizens, and classmates as they shared what it meant to be part of something that changed the course of civil rights. One intriguing aspect was the reaction by present-day students of Clinton High

School as they viewed the film, many of whom had never even heard of the history-making events. Expressions of surprise, even anger, flickered across their faces as they witnessed the harassment endured by these African-American students.

The film revealed the raw hatred, the slurs, the protests, the vandalism, the inflammatory speeches, the KKK threats. One picture showed a smiling boy in a crowd, holding a sign that read: "We won't go to school with Negroes!" There was a deafening silence as the young audience learned the details of the 1958 bombing, an explosion that nearly destroyed the entire school, after which students had to be transferred to another school while CHS was being rebuilt.

The current students seemed relieved as they watched how Oak Ridge High, a neighboring school, welcomed the students —all of them, black and white alike. The Oak Ridge band played the CHS alma mater as students got off the bus to attend temporary classes there. I personally was touched to learn about this small Tennessee town that had made a huge impact on history.

As ugly as it was, this is a success story. There were people, black and white, who made a difference during this first test of segregation. Brave kids, parents, teachers, and families who did the right thing in spite of those who preached hatred and racism.

There are some battles for which we must stand and fight. Heroes are those who fight for causes that must not fail. The Clinton "12" fought for such a cause.

Heroes Know What They Believe

The way heroes live their lives is determined by their code of behavior, acts of honor or dishonor, and tenets they will live (or die) by. What we believe is passed to our children and grandchildren as they see us living out what we truly believe.

Our country's heroes are men and women who knew what they believed. They set their priorities and did not vacillate between opinions. General George S. Patton is an American World War II military hero because he was such a man. The tall, terse, war wizard became known by his nickname, "Old Blood and Guts," for his dogged pursuit of the enemy and relentless efforts in battle. He turned a ragtag division, once the laughing stock of the Army, into a well-oiled military machine displaying exemplary discipline and valor. The swashbuckling image of Patton standing in his jeep, shaking his fist and daring German fliers overhead to shoot him, is legendary. He expected his men to dress impeccably, carry themselves confidently, behave as gentlemen, and to display extraordinary courage at all times.

Many may not realize that General Patton overcame severe childhood dyslexia to become one of our brightest, most educated, and brilliant military leaders. He referred to his time of service to our country as his "rendezvous with destiny." One UPI reporter offered this eulogy in tribute to the four-star general: "General George S. Patton believed he was the greatest soldier who ever lived. He made himself believe he would never falter through doubt. This absolute faith in himself as a strategist and master of daring infected his entire army, until the men of second American corps in Africa, and later, the third army in France, believed they could not be defeated under his leadership." What wonderful insight into a true American hero.

I consider many of our military leaders true heroes—among them former presidents Dwight D. Eisenhower and George Herbert Walker Bush. President Bush was awarded the Navy's Distinguished Flying Cross for "heroism and extraordinary achievement." Many people do not realize that our 41st president was shot down in 1944 on a bombing mission and rescued by a submarine.

Heroes are men and women whose belief in God and country never waver. They believe that everything good and right and just will finally prevail, no matter the cost or the odds.

Heroes Are the Real Deal

People, especially today's young people, see through anyone who is fake. As the saying goes, "It is better to be hated for who you are than to be loved for someone you are not." Heroes are honest, transparent people who never attempt to be anything other than who they are. American writer Carol Lynn Pearson wrote, "Heroes take journeys, confront dragons, and discover the treasure of their true selves."

I meet genuine heroes everywhere I go—at concerts, fundraising events, Wounded Warrior meetings, in airports, hotel lobbies, the grocery store, at church, or at my sons' school activities. They are real men and women who have served or are serving in our armed forces—heroes all.

Just recently I was asked to perform at another "Welcome Home" event for the commanding general and the 101st Army division at Fort Campbell. The Army installation straddles the borders of Tennessee and Kentucky. As the men and women march in and stand at attention in uniform, my feeling is always the same—immense pride and gratitude for their service. Seeing their families rush toward them at the close of the ceremony is a moment every American should witness at least once. I dare anyone to observe such love and show of support without a tear or two —simply impossible.

A few years back Kim and I attended the movie premier of "Pearl Harbor," starring Ben Affleck, Josh Hartnett, and Kate Beckinsale. The premiere was held on the USS Stennis in Pearl Harbor and I was brought in as a surprise guest. Faith Hill sang the theme song from the film, then the movie was shown. As it ended, the screen was raised and I was in place to sing "God Bless the U. S. A.," accompanied by the Honolulu symphony. It was surreal to look over and see the USS *Arizona* Memorial in the distance. Also on stage were surviving veterans of the Pearl Harbor attack.

During the event, one of the most touching and unique moments I have ever experienced occurred when an older man stepped up to play "Taps" in honor of the young men who had died during the Japanese attack. This man had been a sailor aboard one of the ships docked in the harbor that fateful day. The bugle he played that evening was the same bugle he had played on the morning of

December 7, 1941. As he finished, it was a sacred moment, almost like a prayer. The audience was transfixed by this tribute to those who perished on the "day that will live in infamy."

I have met men and women who have served in every war since World War II. I shake the hands of these real-life heroes and say, "Thank you for your service to our country." But it never feels like enough. One song has given me the opportunity to be in the company of these heroes in uniform and I am grateful. We owe these genuine heroes so much.

Heroes See Options Others Don't

Life presents many moments when a decision can not only affect our own lives but the lives and well-being of others. Heroes may not always choose the easiest or most popular path. At times, heroes may even have to stand alone. They stay true to themselves and their own set of values even when others misunderstand or criticize their actions. Heroes forge ahead, often taking the less traveled road, because they understand it is the best possible option.

America first heard the reports on Sunday night, May 1st, 2011. Information was just trickling in about a daring raid on a compound in Pakistan. A United States SEAL team had identified and killed America's public enemy #1, Osama Bin Laden, who had been hiding in the compound for more than five years. We all hung on every word, hoping to hear none of our own young men had been injured or killed in the raid. Finally, the answer came—not one American life was lost or harmed. My mind flashed back to another Navy SEAL team, not so fortunate.

On June 28, 2005, Navy Lt. Michael Murphy and three fellow SEALs were searching for Taliban insurgents on a craggy mountainside in Kunar Province, Afghanistan. After rappelling down from a helicopter the night before, then climbing through a heavy downpour, they established a lookout point high above a village nearby. Everything changed when three local goat herders stumbled upon the SEALs' campsite and were quickly taken as prisoners. A decision to determine the herders' fate altered the mission and ultimately cost many lives. The SEALs' team was made up of Lt. Murphy from Patchogue, New York; Petty Officers Marcus Luttrell from Huntsville, Texas; Danny Dietz of Littleton, Colorado; and Matthew Axelson of Cupertino, California.

There were tense moments as the Americans discussed the rules of engagement and the fate of the captured goat herders. If the goat herders were Taliban sympathizers, they would most assuredly warn the Taliban of the SEALs' presence in the area if set free. On the other hand, killing the herders, while perhaps ensuring the SEALs' safety, had military and media implications, which might even include possible military charges.

Lt. Murphy finally convinced the team that letting the goat herders go would probably be the most humane and politically safe decision. Among the captured herders was a fourteen-year-old boy. Murphy had a younger brother who was approximately fourteen at that time, and that fact could have weighed heavily on him as the team agreed finally to release the prisoners. They all knew the risk, but could not have foreseen the outcome that came so swiftly and violently.

Within an hour, more than one hundred Taliban fighters, armed with grenades and AK-47 assault rifles, descended upon the SEALs. A higher point up the mountain gave the Taliban a huge advantage as they opened fire and sent the SEALs sliding, crawling, tumbling down the mountain, seeking cover. Lt. Murphy continued to direct the team even after suffering a shot to the stomach early in the fight. While taking out many of the Taliban fighters, the SEALs realized they were hopelessly outnumbered.

In his book, *Seal of Honor,* author Gary Williams recounted the story as told by the lone survivor of the operation, Marcus Luttrell. Luttrell remembered the moment when three of the team members had suffered at least one bullet wound and Lt. Murphy took decisive action. With the radio out of commission, he grabbed the satellite phone and stepped out into the open to report the situation to Bagram Airfield base and call for rescue. He was shot again, but managed to complete the phone call with the words, "Roger that, thank you."

In two hours, Murphy, along with Axelson and Dietz, would be dead. The tragic day grew worse when the rescue helicopter, a Chinook MH-47, was shot down by a rocket-propelled grenade. Eight members of the "Night Stalkers," the U.S. Army's elite group, and eight additional SEALs aboard, were killed.

Luttrell alone eluded death and capture and was taken in by villagers nearby who hid him until he was rescued by Special Forces five days later. He has some regret over the decision to spare the herders, but understands the decision at that time was based on the fact that their captives were clearly civilians. He remembers Murphy as his best friend.

The USS *Michael Murphy*, named after the Medal of Honor recipient, is a sleek, new, ultra-modern warship that was christened on May 7, 2011, the day Lt. Murphy would have been thirty-five years old. While we celebrate the actions and the outcome of the Navy SEALs who ridded the world of bin Laden, I celebrate another heroic SEAL team who died on a mountain somewhere deep in Afghanistan because they showed mercy on some civilian goat herders. Heroes weigh options, then act in ways that support their deepest, most valued convictions.

Heroes Choose Love and Honor

As I study the lives of the patriarchs of our faith like Abraham, Moses, and Elijah, I see them as heroes, too. These were common men, made great through the discipline of their faith and trust in God. God enabled and gifted these men for the unique times and tasks for which He had called them.

One of my favorite heroes of the Bible is Joseph. His story reads like a modern-day novel filled with all the elements of human conflict: hatred, jealousy, brokenness, then finally restoration and forgiveness.

Think about it: God gave Joseph some divine dreams, promises of elevation and honor so great they were hard to believe. When Joseph revealed the dreams to his brothers, they hated him, sold him into slavery, and told their father he was dead. Then, after gaining favor in his master's home, Joseph was accused of rape and sat in prison for years for a crime he did not commit. Were there times when Joseph doubted God, his future, even the dream? Every negative circumstance Joseph encountered only made him more capable of fulfilling the dream. All along, God had Joseph in hero training. He was honing him to be a ruler in the very throne room of Egypt.

The Bible is full of heroes we can emulate, none so important as Jesus, who lived an exemplary life, died a horrible death to prove His love for mankind, then was gloriously resurrected. The Bible declares that one day, "every knee shall bow and every tongue confess that Jesus Christ is Lord" (Phil. 2:10). On that day, whenever it may be, our Lord will be praised and proclaimed as the ultimate Hero.

The heroes among us emulate our Lord when they consciously choose to reject selfishness and consider the needs of others over themselves. It happens in war, in business, in the classroom, in the home. I like to think of it this way: Every day we choose which path we will follow; we will either walk in love or selfishness. The moment we choose to walk in selfishness, we have rejected love and kindness. Same is true of choosing to walk in love. Walking in love immediately makes us aware of others—their needs, hurts, and concerns. There are only two areas we live in—love or selfishness. We are choosing one or the other every day, all day long. Heroes choose to care.

It must be an indescribable moment when the president of the United States places our country's Medal of Honor around the neck of a recipient. That medal, with the beautiful blue ribbon and white stars, stands for heroic actions, selfless deeds, and uncommon valor. May we all seek to live our lives in such a way that if awards were given for devotion to faith, family, and country, we would be worthy of such an honor. God needs heroes; America needs heroes—men and women who meet every crisis, every adversary, and every circumstance in life with heroic actions, selfless deeds, and uncommon valor. Who knows? God may present some medals of His own one day. It may surprise us whom God would select as heroes.

God's greatest heroes may not be the most skilled preachers, the television evangelists ministering to thousands, or the popular rock stars who have prayer with their crews before each show. His hero may not be the businessman who single-handedly gives money to erect the finest church in town, or the head of the deacon board. Instead, God's most honored hero may be the little grandmother who sits alone in a humble home but prays in earnest for the salvation of her family. It may be a tiny child, frightened but hopeful that life will one day provide her with the love she so deserves. God's heroes may include the young athletes who gather mid-field after Friday night football games to unashamedly pray and thank Him for the ability to compete. Real heroes seek one thing—to hear God one day say, "Well done, thou good and faithful servant" (Matt. 25:21).

Heroes Are not Defined by Past Failures

Heroes aren't perfect—some of them have made huge mistakes in the past. But their mistakes did not hamstring them or keep them from trying again. In fact, God uses the most devastating failures to teach us patience, discipline, trust, and faith. It is so sad to see someone defined by some past failure, one who never rose above that one moment, that one poor choice or deed. Heroes are people who refuse to let past mistakes determine who they are or will be.

One of our country's greatest inventors, Thomas Edison, looked like a failure at several points in his life. One of his early teachers declared him to be incapable of learning. His mother began to homeschool him and, for the rest of his life, Edison was self-taught. As a young man he borrowed money for his first laboratory, but soon found himself deeply in debt, bankrupt, and on the verge of starvation. He took a job repairing machinery but was convinced that with enough time and capital, he could invent useful tools for the American public. He borrowed $40,000, established another laboratory, and hired assistants. Month after month, Edison experimented tirelessly, sleeping in a bed set up in his makeshift laboratory. He found some success with the phonograph, moving pictures, telegraph, and telephone improvements. Finally, in 1879, after 1,200 experiments, Edison perfected the incandescent light bulb. That one invention changed America and the world. Entire cities were lit for the first time and Edison became a millionaire almost overnight. He was lauded as the most influential figure of the millennium. Edison was the hero of science and the modern world. But it wasn't easy.

Failure could not stop Edison. In fact, just like other heroes, he learned that only through failure can you learn. He said, "I have not failed. I've just found 10,000 ways that won't work." He also remarked, "Many of life's failures are people who didn't realize how close they were to success when they gave up!" Heroes refuse to allow failure to keep them from their destiny. They shift their thinking, go in another direction, or solve the problem and learn from every failure. Motivational speaker and author, Zig Ziglar is credited with saying, "Failure is an event, not a person." So true. Heroes are those who always give it one more shot.

Heroes Are Ordinary People

There are heroes among us. Ordinary men and women who, as Reagan mentioned following the Challenger disaster, are heroes "for the way they live their lives." These are single moms who sacrifice, sometimes working several jobs to provide for their children; underpaid teachers who pour themselves into their students every day, all for the joy of seeing them learn; firemen and policemen who risk their lives to serve our communities across this country; farmers who toil long hours to harvest crops to feed our growing population; the factory worker and the store clerk who report to work every day, doing their part for our economic systems. They "live their lives" as testimonies of what hard work and dedication can do. These every-day heroes make our nation work and deserve our sincere thanks.

One of my favorite movies of all time is *To Kill a Mockingbird.* Atticus Finch, played by Gregory Peck, is an attorney who tries to win freedom for a black man, Tom Robinson, falsely accused of rape. The jury in the southern town convicts Tom even when Atticus presents evidence to the contrary. As they lead him away follow-ing the verdict, Atticus promises Tom that he will start the appeal process the next morning. In the balcony are several members of the black community who have come to see Atticus defend their friend.

Jean Louise, Atticus's daughter, nicknamed "Scout," is also seated in the balcony. The courtroom empties and Atticus gathers his papers and begins to walk dejectedly down the aisle toward the doors of the courthouse. Suddenly, but reverently, the men and women in the balcony stand in a show of respect for Atticus, even though many are shaken by the outcome. The black Reverend Sykes turns to Scout and says, "Miss Jean Louise, stand up—your father's passing."

The scene chokes me up every time. We all need other human beings to affirm us, to support us, to believe in us. But when all is said and done, to live a life that garners respect and admiration from those who know you best is to reach a pinnacle one can only hope to achieve. To be considered worthy of honor from those who see you everyday amid ordinary or extraordinary challenges is the finest affirmation one can attain.

I close this chapter realizing I may never be considered a hero in the eyes of the world, but I am asking God to make me a hero in the eyes of my wife and sons. They are *my* heroes. Walter Schirra wrote, "You don't raise heroes, you raise sons. And if you treat them like sons, they'll turn out to be heroes, even if it's only in your own eyes."

So, who will be the heroes for our children? I am concerned when I read how rap stars, gang members, and arrogant sports figures are idolized. My hope is that as each generation matures, they model them-selves after those who are honest, law-abiding, caring, respectful contributors to our American way of life. We may never see their names in print. They may not be publicly recognized, nor garner the praise of thousands. They just go about their lives making the right choices, desiring fairness, striving to be the best wife, mother, father, son, worker, soldier, boss, foreman, church member, American they can be.

Where are the heroes? Right here. Among us.

Thanks for "God Bless the U.S. A."

Dear Lee,

I served on a Navy destroyer (USS Coontz DDG-40). Whenever we would come back from an extended cruise, the families would be waiting for us at the pier, waving American flags and your song, "God Bless the U.S.A." would be playing on a sound system. We could hear it from the ship as we approached the pier.

The song held particular meaning for us when we arrived home from a particularly long and difficult deployment to the Persian Gulf in 1987. We had been patrolling the Persian Gulf during the Iran/Iraq War, ensuring safe passage for oil tankers leaving the Gulf and relaying information on Iraqi jet movements. On May 14, an Iraqi Mirage fighter jet flew an attack pattern on a merchant ship, taking it dangerously close to the USS Coontz. Our captain warned the pilot by radio if he came closer, he would be fired upon. The jet eventually turned away.

We returned to port two days later because we were running low on fuel. The USS Stark left the next morning to take our place on patrol at an operating area known as RPS South. It seemed like any other typical day as we watched the Stark leave port. Twelve hours later, an Iraqi jet fired to Exocet missiles at the Stark. The first missile went entirely through the ship. The second entered the Stark, but the warhead didn't explode. However, it spewed burning rocket fuel into the ship. Thirty-seven crew members of the Stark died in the attack.

A couple of days later, a memorial service was held at the Bahrain International Airport. As a Navy journalist, my job was to photograph the event. A few of the caskets containing the deceased crew members had already been loaded into the back of the cargo plane for transport. I climbed into the plane to take photos of the flag-draped coffins. As I stood looking at the name tags attached to them it struck me that I had come close to being in one of those boxes, with my name on a tag. The actions of my captain, our return to port due to low fuel, the USS Stark taking our place at RPS-South and the grace of God kept that from happening.

My ship was among those that escorted the Stark home after repairs were made to make her stable enough to get under way. When we returned to the United States, we were greeted by a huge crowd. "God Bless the U.S.A." was playing loud and clear from the pier. The crew of the Coontz "manned the rails" in our summer white uniforms as the ship slowly made its way in. We were happy to finally be home, but there were tears as we heard that song, especially the words, "there ain't no doubt I love this land …." I had been on several deployments in the Navy, but I had never been happier or prouder to return home and your song was there to greet us. Every time I hear "God Bless the U.S.A." I think of my time in the Persian Gulf, the hours we spent at general quarters, our close call at RPS-South, and the brave men of the USS Stark.

—Terry Cordingley, September 2011
Mustang, Oklahoma

Does God Still Bless the U.S.A.?

It is summer now and Nashville has exploded with flowers rich in colors found only in the south. Magnolia trees are blooming in neighborhoods lining Music Row and from my back patio I catch a slight scent of jasmine floating in the air. Eight months have passed since I set out to ask this question in book form, "Does God Still Bless the U.S.A.?" This book may or may not be the last one I write, but, there will never be one that is more important to me. People raise their eyebrows when I tell them the title of the new book, "Does God Still Bless the U.S.A.?" They look at me as if to ask, "Well, does He?"

Before I offer my summation on all we have discussed, let me reiterate how much I love this country. A Leon Russell song starts with these words, "I've been so many places in my life and time ...." The song must have had me in mind. I've traveled by bus from coast to coast more times than I can count, flown into the tiniest and largest airports, 'have sang in every outhouse, doghouse, and roundhouse' and I can honestly say every part of America is special to me.

I've experienced cold, icy winters in Minnesota, stifling summers in southwest Texas, rodeo arenas in small towns, and ornate concert halls in our largest cities. I have sung for Kiwanis clubs, county fairs, labor unions, and presidents. I have performed for events to benefit victims of disease, war, and national disasters such as hurricanes, tornados, floods and fires all over this nation. I've met generals and foot soldiers, housewives and superstars, traveled to many countries of the world and I say this without hesitation; there is no place like home. This place we call home, however, is in need of some attention, some deliberate maintenance for the future. This is why I felt compelled to write this book.

I remember one particular night while working in Vegas at The Golden Hotel with my band, The Apollos. I was only sixteen but I already had a world of experience behind me. When the curtain opened we didn't realize it was still ten more feet to the lip of the stage. My guitar player grabbed his microphone to move it forward for the opening number and didn't notice the cord from his guitar to the amplifier was too short. The amplifier was jerked from the drum riser with a loud crash and the tubes inside fell out onto the stage. What an entrance! We knew we needed that amplifier, so while the bass player and drummer kept playing and the audience roared with laughter, Eddie Lovato and I scrambled around on the floor, trying to put the thing back together. It was a mess. I was all thumbs trying to get the tubes back in the amplifier, attempting to match the right pins in the right holes, working frantically to get it to work so the show could continue. Somehow, we got it in place again, but needless to say, it wasn't the suave, cool beginning we had planned for.

In similar fashion, I wonder if some Americans are working frantically to keep the country intact while others, like our Vegas audience that night, sit back wondering if the ones on stage will ever get it right. Is there a majority of citizens who want America to succeed? (They want to see the show, but never think of getting involved). I hope this book makes people aware of the bigger picture at stake.

Walk into any large mall or building and you immediately see a map. On the map is usually a red star with the words,, "You are here." The map is provided to give the visitor a sense of direction or perspective. Essentially, I am asking you to take a look at where you are in the picture of America's future. Your decision will determine

God's blessings for our country. Will we change who we are in the upcoming decades, or will we strive to remain focused on values God established for mankind from the beginning?

It is time to choose … you are here!

—Lee

America's story is too big for any movie screen and no American history book can do it justice. It is like a marvelously scripted play.

Act I highlights a tenuous beginning, a battle for independence and the right to exist; then glorious victory.

Act II is high drama as the new nation is nearly ripped apart with internal conflict between the states, followed by a period of peace and restoration.

Act III begins as outside aggression thrusts her into two World Wars which threaten her future and the future of the entire world, followed again, by glorious victory. She also must survive the effects of world wide depression in 1929. In the coming years, America's ingenuity and new inventions catapult her to the forefront as technology advances.

Act IV features a race for world dominance in the areas of nuclear power, space exploration, and economic stability. Two more wars during this period, in Korea and Vietnam, influenced the mood of the country.

The final acts have yet to be written. America has entered a war against terrorism in response to the attacks of 9/11. We are also currently experiencing economic turmoil and political distrust. No one can determine how events will play out in the coming years. But here is the important question: what will your role be in this grand script? We all have a role to play, whether we realize it or not. If you are American, you have a part to play. Every generation has added their own act to the script, and we are writing ours as we speak.

In 1989 I received a direct call from President Herbert Walker Bush who asked me to organize a USO trip to entertain our military personnel in Panama. The Air Force flew our group from the United States to Panama. Upon landing, the band was taken by Chinook helicopters to the first of three locations where we would perform our shows. I had a letter from the President that I was to deliver to two hundred marines who were deep in the jungle. I was assigned a military escort who picked me up in an Army jeep. As we were traveling through the jungle on a dirt road, we came under enemy fire. A bullet took off the index finger of my driver's right hand. I wrapped his wounded finger in a makeshift tourniquet and we continued to the destination outpost. My heart was beating so fast and loudly, I could hear it in my ears. It happened in seconds but the incident made an eternal impact on my perspective.

Here is what I learned with clarity that day; this is the role I have been called to play for my country. I had always known I had an important part in encouraging and lifting up soldiers here at home and abroad, but an ominous reality settled in. I have never been fearful in situations overseas, but I realized I could have died that day. Then the questions came: Does your country mean that much to you? Would you be willing to die for her? The answer came even while I was still shaken from the experience. If I died while performing my role, so be it. If I had perished in that thick, steamy jungle, it was part of the script, written long before I was born. At that moment, I established in my heart, no matter the cost, that I would stand in the grandest arenas before thousands or on street corners where only two or three might hear, for the privilege of singing, God Bless the U. S. A. for as long as I'm able. I feel it is my duty as a believer and as an American to live out this role faithfully for as long as I can do so.

Other roles I relish, given to me before time began, are those of husband and father. I will live my life with no question as to where my priorities lie. My wife will never doubt my love or devotion to her. I live to see her smile and to know that she feels treasured and precious to me beyond any earthly possession. I vow to see my sons safely and wisely delivered into adulthood with every tool they need to succeed, never questioning my unconditional love or respect.

These are my roles. What are yours? Never underestimate your part in this story called America.

So here are my final thoughts on the question framed in the title of this book, "Does God Still Bless the U.S.A.?"

Does God Still Bless the U.S.A.?
Yes! In the Same Way He Blesses all Mankind

God yearns for us to know Him intimately, all of us, every single human being. Many will seek life's answers though various means, but hopefully, before the final curtain they will come to know that God alone is all they need and all they have been searching for. This is the basis for answering the question, "Does God Still Bless the U.S.A.?" First of all, God blesses us because we are His creation and He chose to "shed His grace" on America along with all humanity.

I can hear some of you saying, "But, Lee, many Americans exclude God from their lives, some even deny His existence. We are not the same Christian nation that formed our basic society in the early days of our history. We have strayed far from the Christian principles that governed us. Will God still bless us even though many among us, including pseudo-intellectuals, view Him as irrelevant? Will He bless us when so many of these individuals control the airwaves and media outlets? Will He continue to bless us when many ignore, even reject the very love He offers?"

I believe He will because God will *always* have a remnant of believers. There are still strong, unwavering, deeply committed men and women who keep America tied to the Almighty, praying ceaselessly, believing for her highest good, living to honor and praise Him in all things.

You may recall the story of the prophet, Elijah in the Old Testament. He is at a low point in his life, tired, and feeling defeated when He goes before God to complain, "I have been very zealous for the Lord God of hosts; because the children of Israel have forsaken Your covenant, torn down Your altars, and killed Your prophets with the sword. *I alone am left*; and they seek to take my life," (I Kings 11:14).

God comforted Elijah, gave him direction, then closed with this word to him, "Yet I have reserved seven thousand in Israel; all whose knees have not bowed to Baal...," (I Kings 11:18). In other words, God assured Elijah that *he was not alone.*

Later in Roman 11:3 of the New Testament, Apostle Paul remembers the account and says, "So, too at the present time there is a remnant, chosen by grace."

I, too, am confident there are thousands upon thousands of God-fearing, Bible believing, sold-out Christians, "chosen by grace," who are pleading for America's soul and her future everyday! They stand firmly between us and the forces of darkness that seek to destroy us. We owe them everything. Above all, *they* are the reason God still blesses the U.S.A.

> "Not until I went into the churches of America and heard her pulpits flame with righteousness did I understand the secret of her genius and power. America is great because America is good, and if America ever ceases to be good, America will cease to be great."
>
> —Alexis de Tocqueville

Does God Still Bless the U.S.A.?

Yes, Because He Loves Freedom!

I love the state motto for New Hampshire that appears on their car tags. It says, "Live Free or Die." As a "free society" what do we believe the word freedom to mean? Webster defines freedom as: a) the absence of necessity, coercion, or constraint in choice or action, or, b) liberation from slavery or restraint or from the power of another. With that said, perhaps we should discuss what freedom is not. Freedom is not the ability to do just whatever we want to do whenever we want to do it. It isn't just going to the polls and voting, although that is an important part of a free democracy. It isn't the flippant pursuit of any or every unbridled pleasure. Freedom doesn't mean we are free to do just anything, but we are free to do the *right* thing.

As part of what is referred to as the "free world," Americans speak of freedom often; it is our way of life. It is the single most important fiber of our American culture which many have fought for, even died for. Our freedom was won by founding fathers who established the country on the right to be free. Every good American feels the necessity of maintaining freedom for future generations. It is part of our DNA, it's who we are and one of our greatest attributes as a civilization. We are free men and women guaranteed certain freedoms by the Constitution; the freedom to speak, to bear arms, and to worship as we please, among others.

Freedom originated with God when he created man with a free will. That free will was apparent when Adam chose to disobey God in the Garden of Eden. God does not demand or desire love if it is forced or expected. This is why He created man with a capacity to determine his own fate—to choose to love and follow Him, or not.

The theme of freedom was also apparent through out the ministry of Jesus while here on earth. As purported in the New Testament, everywhere He went, people were set free: free from death, free from disease, free from suffering, free from their past, and free from sin. The New Testament gospel is that theme in a nutshell: "Therefore, whom the Son sets free, shall be free indeed," (John 8:36).

Our free will is paramount to God. He has placed within man the intense desire to oppose any attempt to enslave his mind, his body, his spirit, or hinder the pursuit of his dreams. I believe God will continue to "bless the U.S.A." because he knows the American people are determined, resourceful, and resilient. No matter the difficulty, whether it be war, political upheaval, or tough economic times, we must remain staunch defenders of freedom and equality. I suggest we return to those same principles of faith that defined us in the beginning and those that I pray will endure for generations to come. When the pilgrims landed at Plymouth Rock they brought their inheritance of faith with them.

I have no doubt, as long as our country is dedicated to equality, justice, and individual rights, God will continue to bless us in the future.

Does God Still Bless the U.S.A.?

Yes! He has Proven It Again and Again

When asking, "Does God Still Bless the U.S.A.?" let's remember how God has blessed her time and again in the past. How did farmers and boys barely old enough to hold a musket, get the best of Britain's most decorated generals in the Revolutionary War? How did we survive without faith during the War Between the States, the deadliest war in our history, which took the lives of 618,000 men? There was an enormous cost, but the union was preserved.

I believe it was the mercy of God that saw us through the first World War which could have ended in disaster at home and abroad. Then, on the heels of recovering from war, the world was impacted by economic crisis. How did the United States survive the economic disaster stemming from the stock market crash of 1929 and the Great Depression that followed? Other nations saw bankruptcy, drought, starvation, and death in staggering numbers. Was it divine intervention that gave President Roosevelt the principles for establishing "the New Deal," a plan that put thousands to work, stabilized our banks, and brought our country out of depression?

During America's recovery from this tough time, a hypnotic personality in Germany began to preach about a "new world order," led by the Aryan race. Adolph Hitler and his Third Reich put a plan in place for world domination. The sinister Nazi symbol began to appear everywhere in Germany. In 1939, Germany invaded Poland and also began a bombardment of Great Britain, putting the world on notice that war was underway. Germany was joined by Italy in 1940 and Japan in 1941. America entered the war following the surprise Japanese attack at Pearl Harbor on December 7, 1941.

Thank God, again the outcome was victory for the Allied Forces. I say this knowing every family in America prayed to God that war would never come to our shores. How is it that we are the only country within the allied nations that never had to defend our own native soil? France, Great Britain, Russia all saw fighting within their borders—not the U.S.A. Also the enemy nations of Germany, Japan, and Italy saw death and destruction at home—not America. Could we have been chosen before time to defend democracy and freedom in far away places like Guadalcanal, Iwo Jima, Ardennes, and Normandy? The sacrifice of 420,000 American lives insured the safety of our sacred homeland. I feel God indeed protected us from the devastation experienced by other countries who were involved during World War II. Until September 11, 2001, the United States had never been attacked here at home. This made that tragic event even more devastating and reprehensible to the collective American soul.

Here's another point for thought. How has the world, the United States included, averted nuclear holocaust? During the Cold War, Americans were made aware of the "red phone" that could be used by our President to direct the release of nuclear missiles aimed at Cuba or Russia. Did nations owning this incredible capability suddenly grow a conscience and see the utter insanity of nuclear warfare? Or was a greater power at work to convince men they could annihilate each other within seconds. As more nations develop the technology to produce nuclear weapons, including mid-eastern countries in turmoil, I believe only God can continue to protect us from this kind of global threat.

It is not my contention that God loves America more than other nations around the world, but why do you suppose we have been spared catastrophes affecting other countries? Many countries have suffered unparalleled suffering and loss of life due to earthquakes, tsunamis, floods, and famine. Many of these events take place in underdeveloped countries where there is little or no plan for preparedness or prevention, but don't you agree we have been blessed even in those respects? I admit, we have had our share of tornadoes, floods, and hurricanes, even earthquakes, but loss of life is minimal compared to statistics resulting from natural disasters in other parts of the world. God continues to bless us in this way. Thank you, God.

Does God Still Bless the U.S.A.?

Yes! Because He Answers Prayer

In 1918 Irving Berlin wrote a powerful song entitled, "God Bless America." When it was presented, the song was part of a musical review and didn't receive much attention. However, later as the United States entered World War II, the song was re-released and immediately embraced by the country. Most who heard it first, heard it as a prayer for God to bless our country with success during the war effort. It is still appreciated and loved and is indeed a prayer for God's blessing. Of course, just saying (or singing) "God Bless America" or "God Bless the U.S.A." does not make it a prayer—it has to be a heart felt plea from one's heart to God; a prayer of faith.

Can you think of the first time you ever heard the words, "God bless the United States of America?" For as long as I can recall, our nation's presidents, and politicians have used the phrase at the close of speeches. It is such a common tag line some may not give it much thought.

What do we really mean when we invoke God's blessing on our nation? For some, God's blessings mean receiving His protection from our enemies. Others may hear the words as a plea of hope that our nation be prosperous. But, I would say for most of us, it goes deeper. It becomes personal. It reaches a basic level and focuses on God's blessings to us individually. When most of us ask God to bless America, we are really asking, "God bless America by keeping me and my children safe from harm or danger." "God bless America by giving my family economic stability." "God, bless America by helping people get jobs and bless those who need Your help most." In essence, we are saying, "Please God, bless America, and bless me, too."

Does God still bless the U.S.A.? Again yes, because God answers prayer, whether it is the prayer of a father whose son is serving in the military, a sweet child kneeling beside her bed, a longshoreman working the docks of New York, or the president of the United States. Every time those words are whispered, shouted, or merely thought, I know God hears and responds.

If you asked me, I would tell you God has blessed America through out history to a remarkable degree. His blessings are not measured as most people believe by material affluence or prosperity alone. His blessings go much deeper than maintaining our status as a world power.

The greatest blessings God has given America have been spiritual blessings. From the beginning, our forefathers invoked God's blessings by praying that men and women and children would come to know and believe in Christ. Salvation through Christ was not only preached from pulpits, but also spoken in the halls of Congress, on the steps of the United States Capitol, and from the lips of presidents from George Washington onward. Our nation was made a fertile place for the gospel to be propagated; men of faith invoked God's blessings for spiritual prosperity in our new nation. If God continues to bless the U.S.A., it will be because America again expects our leaders to be men and women of clean character and moral conviction.

I want to be clear. I don't believe external moral reform alone makes America deserving of God's blessings. Something deeper is needed in our lives. Merely reciting the words of my song, "God Bless the U.S.A." will do nothing for us, until it becomes a fervent prayer for our country's spiritual renewal. Political remedies will not be enough in the future. We need to embrace the only truth that can genuinely set people free. Laws are necessary and we have the Constitution to ensure individual rights, but laws cannot make people good or righteous. The way we live our lives, not laws will keep God's blessings coming.

After 9/11/01 many asked, "Is God angry with America?" Church attendance rose, interest in spiritual things was rekindled as we tried to figure out what it all meant? Some blamed a trend toward a more sinful, secular society. The remedy to our nation's moral and spiritual woes begins with personal repentance, rather than just pointing fingers at the evils of a secular society. Believers must be examples of their faith, humility and righteousness. God will continue to bless the U.S.A. in response to earnest, prayer for our nation. He promised to do so. "If My people, who are called by My name, will humble themselves, and pray and seek My face, and turn from their wicked ways, then I will hear from heaven and will forgive their sin and heal their land," (II Chronicles 7:14).

Does God Still Bless the U.S.A.?

Yes, Because She is Still That "Shining City on a Hill"

President Ronald Reagan often borrowed a phrase, "shining city on a hill" from a message by John Winthrop. Winthrop was one of the brave, hardy pilgrims who left Britain in search of religious freedom and the pursuit of happiness. He encouraged his fellow newcomers with these words spoken on the deck of the Arabella off the coast of Massachusetts in 1630:

"We shall be a city on a hill. The eyes of all people are upon us so that if we shall deal falsely with our God in this work we have undertaken and so cause Him to withdraw His present help from us, we shall be made a story and a byword throughout the world."

I asked you earlier in this chapter to consider your role in the story called America. Winthrop warned us over three hundred eighty one years ago that the grand story could potentially be one referred to only in past tense if we "deal falsely with God," the result of which would cause Him to "withdraw His help (blessings) from us."

What does that phrase mean: "deal falsely with God?" It means to ridicule or forsake the simple, pure faith of our forefathers for what some call the age of enlightenment. It would mean claiming to be a God-fearing nation, then electing men and women to office who would abuse power and make a mockery of our political system. It would mean neglecting the principles of equality for all men; devaluing the values God holds dear; refusing to teach our children about their spiritual heritage. We must reject ever growing efforts by film makers and those who produce video games to push the limits of decency. We must curtail the sexual rancor and violence in music listened to by our children as well. We must demand the highest standards of behavior for athletes, business executives, and politicians. We must also reject racism of any kind and embrace again our role as a "melting pot," offering freedom for all. Again, we come from many nations, but we are all 100% American.

Remember the map? We are here... and it is time. The moment has come to get off the perch of half-hearted patriotism and watered down faith. Our future will require a firm commitment to all we were established to be, not a timorous nod in God's direction but full out faith in Him. America must decide if she is willing to live by that faith. Either we embrace Him implicitly, trust Him absolutely with our souls and our future, or see our light diminished as a once "shining city on a hill." It is time to shout from the highest rooftops, "In God We *Still* Trust!"

And for as long as that remains true, yes, God Will Bless the U.S.A.!

The stage lights dim for the last song; always the show's finale. I hear the introduction playing for "God Bless the U.S.A." the song

I have been singing for decades now. I haven't bothered to count how many times I've sung the song. One day I will add them all up, maybe when I am unable to sing anymore. The audience recognizes the first few notes and some people stand even before I begin to sing. I check myself: "Sing from your heart. Sing like it is the first time you have sung it. Deliver the song like this is the first time anyone has heard it. Feel it, believe it, pray it."

"If tomorrow all the things were gone I'd worked for all my life…"

Thanks for "God Bless the U.S. A."

What is a community? I found an answer recently 30,000 feet over New York City.

En route to Boston October 7th after a visit to Chattanooga, Tennessee, my wife and I had a layover at the Charlotte, North Carolina airport. While waiting for our U.S. airways flight, we caught the latest news program on a large-screen TV in the passengers' lounge.

The images and the words told the story:

U. S. planes were bombing Afghanistan and we were to board a plane back to Boston within the hour. We did so, but with trepidation. And we had a lot of company. The plane was full of nervous travelers just like us.

Some time into the trip, the chief flight attendant announced on the intercom that we would soon be passing over New York City. I thought she might call for a moment of silence for the victims of the Sept 11 World Trade Center attacks. Instead, she announced that singer-songwriter Lee Greenwood, whose song, "God Bless the U.S.A." has been featured in venues throughout this land for the past month, was on board and had offered to sing it for us as we passed over Manhattan.

From six miles up, the five boroughs of New York City were spread out before us. I could barely discern the tip of lower Manhattan where the unthinkable had occurred almost four weeks before. And Lee Greenwood was on the plane's intercom singing:

If tomorrow all the things were gone I'd worked for all my life …

On his third time through, it seemed as if the entire plane had joined in the chorus almost as one. We were not one, however. We were many and diverse. I could see we were black, yellow, brown and white: I suspected we were Muslim, Christian, Jew, Hindu and other belief systems: and we were young, old and in the middle—we had more differences than similarities.

But for an inspirational moment—while rescue workers labored six miles below us in the smoldering ruins of once great buildings, while bombs fell in Afghanistan and more people died, while Lee Greenwood sang to us of patriotism–we were a community united by common experiences and emotions. A community is what you share with others.

—Article by John P. Kinney,
President and Publisher of Essex County Newspapers
Appeared in The Evening News, Salem,
Massachusetts, October 16, 2001

Special thanks...

First, I'd like to thank my wife, the love of my life and partner in everything, Kimberly Payne Greenwood, for being the Senior Editor on this project. This book has been a labor of love for both of us as we have relived the last twenty years of our lives together. Kim devoted many late nights and time away from her own business, pouring over pages of dialogue to help me organize my thoughts. Thank you, honey. I couldn't have authored this book without you and will always cherish our *Prayers of a Patriot*.

Secondly, I would like to thank my Line Editor, Ann Severance, for her consistent input from a biblical perspective and for making sure all the "t's" were crossed and the "i's" were dotted. Kim and I are convinced that God brought you into our lives and we are amazed by your work ethic. Thank you, Ann, for being such a gracious lady and for your powerful biblical knowledge and recommendations. You are a blessing in my life.

Lastly, I would like to thank Mrs. Rita Tate, my Creative Project Manager. Rita was tolerant of my entertainment schedule and made time available whenever I needed, to discuss every chapter in detail. Her style of writing and depth of vocabulary was invaluable to the text. Thank you, Rita for being my guide on this project. I am proud to call you my friend.

—Lee Greenwood

30-Day Devotional Guide

Prayers of a Patriot

by Lee and Kim Greenwood

It is our hope that this Devotional Guide will inspire you and your family to pray everyday for our homes, our leaders, our world, and our beloved America.

—Lee and Kim

Day 1

Pray for Marriage—Your Own and Others

Dear Heavenly Father,

We are grateful that you brought us together. We love and respect each other deeply and ask that You protect our marriage from the snares of the enemy. While life is busy and the demands on our time are many, we ask that we never suffer from disconnected hearts, which leads to neglect. Help us always to acknowledge that no problem, no obstacle, no challenge is hopeless when brought to You. In all that we do, assist us in putting the importance of our marriage before all else.

Scripture Reference: Genesis 2: 18, 22-24

"The Lord GOD said, 'It is not good for the man to be alone. I will make a helper suitable for him....' Then the Lord GOD made a woman from the rib he had taken out of the man, and he brought her to the man. The man said, 'This is now bone of my bones and flesh of my flesh; she shall be called 'woman,' for she was taken out of man.' For this reason a man will leave his father and mother and be united to his wife, and they will become one flesh."

Day 2

Pray for Your Children

Dear Heavenly Father,

Thank You for the honor of parenting our children. We know that they were perfect in every way when You entrusted them to us. Help us to nurture, love, and direct them so that when they come to adulthood, they serve You with all their hearts and minds. Please guide them in making life decisions. We pray today for their future spouses, wherever they are in the world. Help them to be brought up in loving, Christian homes that they may share the same values of faith, family, and country. Please lead the steps of our children so that they never suffer from indecision. Give them wisdom and an everlasting joy that ultimately comes from serving You all the days of their lives.

Scripture Reference: Psalm 127:3-5

"Children are a heritage from the LORD, the fruit of the womb is His reward. Like arrows in the hand of a warrior, so are the children of one's youth. Happy is the man who has his quiver full of them."

Day 3

Pray for Our Soldiers and Military Leaders

Dear Heavenly Father,

Thank You for the brave men and women who protect the freedom of the United States of America every day. They are our heroes. We ask, Lord, that You keep them safe. You know where they are throughout the world, and You know the aggression and the hardships they face. We ask You to protect them with the strength of Your mightiest angels. We also ask that You give our military leaders wisdom. Guide their decisions as they collectively work toward peace through strength...and may they always feel the appreciation of the country they protect.

Scripture Reference: Psalm 91:2, 3, 5-7

"I will say of the Lord, 'He is my refuge and my fortress, my God, in whom I trust.' Surely he will save you from the fowler's snare...You will not fear the terror of night, nor the arrow that flies by day....A thousand may fall at your side, ten thousand at your right hand, but it will not come near you."

Day 4

Pray for the President and National Legislators (Senate, Congress)

Dear Heavenly Father,

Thank You for a country where every voice is heard and valued and every vote is counted! We ask You, Lord, to guide the president of the United States, along with our Senate and Congress. We ask, Lord, that they always put the greater good of our nation before any political posturing or struggle for control. You have gifted our leaders with great character, great intellect, wisdom, and strength. We ask that our leaders use these traits to serve our nation, its citizens, and its future with every fiber of their being.

Scripture Reference: Psalm 72:1, 2, 4

"Endow the king with your justice, O God, the royal son with your righteousness. He will judge your people in righteousness, your afflicted ones with justice....He will defend the afflicted among the people and save the children of the needy; he will crush the oppressor."

Day 5

Pray for Your Family's Safety and for the Protection and Safety of Our Nation

Dear Heavenly Father,

We thank You for our beautiful family and our majestic nation. Lord, we feel Your hand of blessing on both. We ask, Lord, for Your protection. We ask that You put a hedge of protection around our family, our nation, and its citizens. Protect us from the evil, destructive schemes of the enemy. As Your Word says, "Be self-controlled and alert. [Our] enemy the devil prowls around like a roaring lion looking for someone to devour" (1 Peter 5:8). Bring us into the bright shining light, where our family and our nation can best serve You.

Scripture Reference: Psalm 141:8-10

"My eyes are fixed on you, O Sovereign Lord; in you I take refuge—do not give me over to death. Keep me from the snares they have laid for me, from the traps set by evildoers. Let the wicked fall into their own nets, while I pass by in safety."

Day 6

Pray for Your Personal Enemies and the Enemies of Our Country

Lord,

Your Word makes it very clear that if we wish to be forgiven for our sins as we stand before You, we must extend forgiveness to our enemies here on earth. Lord, You know who the enemies of our family and our nation are. We pray for them today. May You bring them into the fullness of Your understanding. We pray that hatred, animosity, and destruction are eliminated from the hearts of all men and that the citizens of this world can learn to live together in perfect peace and harmony.

Scripture Reference: Matthew 5:44. 45

"But I tell you: Love your enemies and pray for those who persecute you, that you may be sons of your Father in heaven."

Day 7

Pray for Teachers, Schools, and the Educational System

Dear Loving Father,

We know how special the hearts and the lives of children are to You. You have encouraged all men to come to You as children without fear or reservation. We are concerned, Lord, for the future of our children. We ask, Lord, that You will strengthen the home of every child in the United States so that each one knows unconditional love and security. Help families to value the importance of a well-rounded education. Help them to manage their time more effectively so that they can concern themselves with the educational future of their children. Lord, we pray for the amazing teachers in our country who are truly called to serve our youth. We lift them up and we ask You to give them strength, focus, and the knowledge that they are creating a better America.

We also ask that our education systems not get caught up with altering history in order to be politically correct. History can speak for itself, and an educated population will know how to discern the truth. Help our youth—the students of our schools—to feel the responsibility to lead our nation valiantly into the future.

Scripture Reference: Psalm 25:4, 5

"Show me your ways, O Lord, teach me your paths; guide me in your truth and teach me, for you are God my Savior, and my hope is in you all day long."

Day 8

Pray for Extended Family (Parents, Siblings, Grandparents, etc.)

Lord,

Thank You for the beauty of family. Thank You for the laughter, the kindness, the encouragement, and the unconditional love found in family. Lord, You knew how difficult life would be at times, and You gave us the family unit to offer support and joy in the face of a sometimes dismal world. We ask You to strengthen every family in America. Where there is unrest, bring peace. Where there is strife, bring unity. Where there is illness, bring healing. Where there is dissension, bring agreement. Bring the American family to a safe place of rest, enjoyment, and strength.

Scripture Reference: Ephesians 6:1, 2

"Children, obey your parents in the Lord, for this is right. Honor your father and mother—which is the first commandment with a promise."

Day 9

Pray for Prosperity for Your Family and the Nation

Dear Heavenly Father,

We thank You for the blessings that You have provided to our family and to our nation. We firmly believe that we enjoy those blessings because of the prayers and the wisdom of our forefathers. Help us to heed the responsibility to make good decisions and a commitment of a prayerful life to bring the future of our family and our nation into even greater blessings and protection. We know with greater prosperity comes greater responsibilities. Guide our decisions to give responsibly to assist those families and nations that are less fortunate.

Scripture Reference: Psalm 112:1-3

"Blessed is the man who fears the Lord, who finds great delight in his commands. His children will be mighty in the land....Wealth and riches are in his house, and his righteousness endures forever."

Day 10

Pray for Your Family's Health

Dear Lord,

We thank You for physical and spiritual health. We are aware that both require nurturing. We ask for Your guidance to lead the family into accurate knowledge about healthy habits. Spiritually: taking the time to learn Your Word, to listen and pray, to surround themselves with wise counsel. Physically: to value exercise and healthy eating habits and to abstain from any substance that would harm their health. Where there is illness, bring healing. Where there is suffering, bring relief. Your Word tells us that our bodies are temples ultimately created to serve and be in relationship with You. We ask for good health so that we can fulfill those purposes to the best of our ability.

Scripture Reference: Isaiah 53:4, 5

"Surely he took up our infirmities and carried our sorrows...and by his wounds we are healed."

Day 11

Pray for Those in Need

Dear Heavenly Father,

We are so grateful that Your Word tells us that you will supply all of our needs according to Your riches in glory. We ask that You extend Your hand of mercy and comfort to the downtrodden. Please provide nourishment for those who are hungry, shelter for those who are homeless, and rest for those who are weary. Please bring discernment to those in our nation with more abundance to know how to best use our time and resources to serve.

Scripture Reference: Isaiah 58:6, 7

"Is not this the kind of fasting I have chosen....Is it not to share your food with the hungry and to provide the poor wanderer with shelter—when you see the naked, that you clothe him?"

Day 12

Pray for Our Spiritual Leaders and Churches

(Missionaries, Priests, and Pastors)

Lord,

We thank You for strong leaders of Your Word—our pastors, priests, missionaries, and Bible study leaders. We thank You for the wisdom You have imparted to them and the truth they speak into all those who will listen. Give them strength. Reward their devotion to You and bring blessings to them and their families in countless measure.

Scripture Reference: Ephesians 6:18

"Pray in the Spirit on all occasions with all kinds of prayers and requests. With this in mind, be alert and always keep on praying for all the saints."

Day 13

Pray for Our Nation's Financial Security (Business Leaders, Banking Industry, Economic Systems, Strength of the Dollar)

Dear Lord,

Please help our nation and its leaders to know that when we realize that all that we have and all that we are belongs to You, then all that You have and all that You are belongs to us. We know that the value of money is not important to You. However, the use of wisely placed resources can provide strength to our nation and those we attempt to serve. Please bring wisdom to our leaders as they make financial decisions that impact the citizens and future of our nation.

Scripture Reference: Matthew 6:33

"Seek first his kingdom and his righteousness, and all these things will be given to you as well."

Day 14

Pray for the Salvation of Others

Dear Heavenly Father,

We thank You that man is so special to You that You would send Your only begotten Son to earth to redeem us that we may live in relationship with You and spend eternity with You. We pray for those who have not accepted Your gift of eternal salvation. Equip all believers with the knowledge and courage to reach out to a fallen world.

Scripture Reference: John 3:17

"For God did not send his Son into the world to condemn the world, but to save the world through him."

Day 15

Pray for Personal Wisdom

Dear Heavenly Father,

We thank You that we can call on You and know that You are always actively involved in the details of our life. We do not ask for earthly wisdom, but for Godly wisdom so that our lives and our actions will bless You and Your kingdom. Please eliminate all confusion and indecision from our lives so that we can have clear direction and purpose. We want to be steadfast and solid in the midst of shifting sands.

Scripture Reference: Proverbs 4:7

"Wisdom is supreme; therefore get wisdom. Though it cost all you have, get understanding."

Day 16

Pray for Your Friends and also for the Friends (Allies) of Our Nation

Dear Lord,

We are grateful for the gift of friendships and allies for our nation. For our friends and allies, we pray for Your fruits of the Spirit: love, joy, peace, patience, kindness, goodness, faithfulness, gentleness and self-control (see Galatians 5: 22, 23).

Scripture Reference: John 15:13

"Greater love has no one than this, that one lay down his life for his friends."

Day 17

Pray for Our Nation's Future Strength and Security

Dear Heavenly Father,

We feel so blessed to live in the United States of America. We love our country and are thankful for the brave men and women You led to form this "shining city on a hill." We ask that You bring strength and security to our land and its citizens, as well as a strong vision for the future so that ultimately we leave to our children and grandchildren an even greater country that we inherited.

Scripture Reference: Psalm 37:39, 40

"The salvation of the righteous comes from the Lord; he is their strength in time of trouble. And the Lord shall help them and deliver them; he shall deliver them from the wicked, and save them, because they trust in him.

Day 18

Pray for the Entertainment Industry

Dear Lord,

We are thankful for the arts and the entertainment industry, which bring enjoyment to so many of our citizens. We ask that you direct the steps of the leaders in music, television, theater, art, dance, and movies and bring a renewed sense of responsibility for the impact their creations have on their impressionable public, specifically the youth of our nation.

Scripture Reference: 1 Samuel 12: 23, 24

"Far be it from me that I should sin against the Lord by failing to pray for you. And I will teach you the way that is good and right. But be sure to fear the Lord and serve him faithfully with all your heart."

Day 19

Pray for the Elderly (and Their Caregivers)

Our most gracious Heavenly Father,

We are so blessed to have received this nation and much of our knowledge from the generations who have gone before us. They are the greatest generation in the world. They have served You and our nation well, and we ask that You honor them with golden years that are truly golden: fruitful, enjoyable and peaceful. Teach us to carefully listen to them, to learn from their lives, their examples, and their wisdom. Please also give strength and joy to those who provide care for them.

Scripture Reference: Isaiah 46:4

"Even to your old age and gray hairs I am he, I am he who will sustain you. I have made you and I will carry you; I will sustain you and I will rescue you."

Day 20

Pray for Your State and Local Political Leaders

Dear Lord,

We are grateful for the men and women You have called to serve our local and state communities. We are aware that our country is only as strong as its weakest links; we pray for no weak links in our local, state, and national governments. Let Your light shine before men (see Matthew 5:16); anoint these courageous leaders and guide their lives and the decisions they make to best serve our nation.

Scripture Reference: 2 Thessalonians 3:5; Mark 12:30

"Now may the Lord direct your hearts....Love the Lord your God with all your heart and with all your soul and with all your mind and with all your strength."

Day 21

Pray for the Sick and Infirm

Dear Lord,

We pray for those among us who may be sick and infirm, along with their caregivers. We offer up this prayer found in Numbers 6:24-26: "The LORD bless you and keep you; the LORD make his face shine upon you, and be gracious to you; the LORD lift up his countenance upon you, and give you peace."

Scripture Reference: James 5:13

"Is any one of you sick? He should call the elders of the church to pray over him and anoint him with oil in the name of the Lord. And the prayer offered in faith will make the sick person well; the Lord will raise him up."

Day 22

Pray for Policemen and Firemen and other Public Servants

Dear God,

We are so thankful for our policeman, firemen, and public servants. We have seen time and time again how they put our citizens before their own personal safety. Thank you for their courage, their dedication, their integrity, and their strength. Give them protection and safety; give them peaceful lives and the reward of knowing that they serve a grateful nation.

Scripture Reference: 1 Peter 2:17

"Show proper respect to everyone: Love the brotherhood of believers, fear God, honor the king."

Day 23

Pray for the End of Wars around the World

Dear Lord,

We are thankful for Your creation of our planet. We know that wars, conflict, unrest, pain, and suffering are not from You and we pray for peace. Your Word tells us that "we wrestle not against flesh and blood, but against principalities, against powers, against the rulers of the darkness of this world, against spiritual wickedness in high places" (Ephesians 6:12). Lead us to a place where our citizens no longer engage with the enemy so that we can live in perfect harmony and order with you.

Scripture Reference: Matthew 5:9

"Blessed are the peacemakers, for they will be called sons of God."

Day 24

Pray for Personal Integrity and Courage

Dear Lord,

We thank You for Your Word, which is a light unto our path, for wise counsel, and for the countless citizens who truly strive to live lives of personal integrity. Lord, we lift up the righteous and ask that You protect them from Satan's wicked web, which brings death and destruction. Help all men to know that "a good tree cannot bring forth evil fruit, neither can a corrupt tree bring forth good fruit" (Matthew 7:18). Bring blessings and a life of strong fulfillment to those who are courageous enough to aspire to lives of integrity.

Scripture Reference: Joshua 1:9

"Be strong and courageous. Do not be terrified; do not be discouraged, for the Lord your God will be with you wherever you go."

Day 25

Pray for Forgiveness

Dear Heavenly Father,

We thank You for Your example of forgiveness because it is one of the hardest things we are called to do. Yet without forgiveness, we cannot stand before You. And without extending forgiveness, we live lives full of bitterness and disappointment. "If we say that we have no sin, we deceive ourselves, and the truth is not in us. If we confess our sins, he is faithful and just to forgive us our sins, and to cleanse us from all unrighteousness"(1 John 1:8, 9). Thank You for Your Grace and forgiveness. Please help all mankind to have hearts that can extend true forgiveness, which will calm disputes, bring peace where there is hostility, and love where hate and wickedness reside.

Scripture Reference: 1 John 1:9

"If we confess our sins, he is faithful and just and will forgive us our sins and purify us from all unrighteousness."

Day 26

Pray for Children Who Are Orphaned,

Homeless, Abused, or in Foster Care

Dear Lord,

We thank You for the beauty of our children and the bright futures we see in their faces. We especially ask for Your gentle compassion for those precious children who are orphaned, homeless, abused, or in foster care. Protect them from all predators that would bring them harm. Bring angels of mercy into their lives to embrace them, to share Your love, Your strength, and Your plan for their futures. Help them to know that You are a strong tower that they can run into and they need not fear, because You are with them.

Scripture Reference: Matthew 19:14

"Jesus said, 'Let the little children come to me, and do not hinder them, for the kingdom of heaven belongs to such as these.'"

Day 27

Pray for the Supreme Court Justices and Our Judicial System

Dear God,

We are grateful for the extended knowledge, integrity, wisdom, and intellect You have given the men and women who serve our nation as Supreme Court Justices and throughout the judicial system. Help them to realize the full weight of their responsibilities each day, always putting their personal agendas behind the good of the nation, upholding the principles our nation was built on by our forefathers.

Scripture Reference: Hosea 12:6

"Return to your God; maintain love and justice, and wait for your God always."

Day 28

Pray for Peace for Our Nation and the World

Dear Lord,

We know that "the things which are impossible with men are possible with God" (Luke 18:27). We give the concept of peace for our nation and for our world to You. Where there is division, bring unity. Where there is hate, bring Your perfect love and understanding. Where there is war, killing, abuse, ridicule, and pain, bring peace. A peace that will allow the lion to lie down with the lamb. A peace that will bring freedom and liberty to the oppressed. A peace that will bring mutual respect, understanding and appreciation to all lands.

Scripture Reference: John 14:27

"Peace I leave with you; my peace I give you. I do not give to you as the world gives. Do not let your hearts be troubled and do not be afraid."

Day 29

Pray for a Cure for Disease and Sickness

Dear God,

We are so thankful for the scholarship and the human insights You have given our great physicians and scientists. We know that you are sensitive to the struggles facing men, women, and children living with life-threatening diseases such as cancer and HIV/AIDS. Hold each of those people a little closer to Your perfect love. Grant them strength and courage. Give our medical community the knowledge to bring cures to these global plagues to end this type of senseless suffering forever.

Scripture Reference: Psalm 103:3

"He forgives all my sins and heals all my diseases; he redeems my life from the pit and crowns me with love and compassion."

Day 30

Pray that America Will Always Acknowledge and

Trust in God as the Source of All Her Blessings

Dear Lord,

We are eternally grateful for the courageous men and women who fled religious persecution to form this new republic. You guided their path. You brought forth a new nation against all odds and honored the lives of those men and women who sought You first. You imparted Your wisdom to those great men and women who are recorded in our history books. This nation we have inherited is strong, in large part, because of Your faithfulness to our forefathers. Lord, we fully acknowledge that You are the source of all our blessings, and we pray for those blessings to be multiplied for each generation.

Scripture Reference: Psalm 33:12

"Blessed is the nation whose God is the Lord, the people he chose for his inheritance."

*Lee with Army personnel during USO Tour
to Afghanistan in September, 2003*

*Lee performing at the commemorative celebration of Ronald
Reagan's 100th birthday at the Ronald Reagan Library*

Greenwood family enjoying a Tennessee Titans football game

Lee and Kim's Wedding Portrait, April, 1992

Dick Chaney and Colin Powell welcomes Lee to platform during the anniversary event for the Persian Gulf War, held on the campus of Texas A & M.

Former President H.W. Bush and Lee have a longstanding relationship—pictured here in 1988

Lee and Kim Greenwood at Muhammad Ali's
Charity Event, Fight Night in 2011.

Lee entertaining fans in his trademark stars and stripes jacket

For Lee Greenwood's Tour Schedule and Special Events see:
www.leegreenwood.com
To order additional copies of
"Does God Still Bless the U.S.A.?"
www.leegreenwood.com
or
www.tatepublishing.com
1-888-361-9473

e|LIVE

listen|imagine|view|experience

TWO SONG AND AUDIO BOOK DOWNLOADS
INCLUDED WITH THIS BOOK!

In your hands you hold a complete digital entertainment package. In addition to the paper version, you receive a free download of the audio version of this book, the song that inspired this book and one additional song. Simply use the code listed below when visiting our website. Once downloaded to your computer, you can listen to the songs and book through your computer's speakers, burn it to an audio CD or save the file to your portable music device (such as Apple's popular iPod) and listen on the go!

How to get your free song download:

1. Visit www.tatepublishing.com and click on the elLIVE logo on the home page.
2. Enter the following coupon code:
   c2a0-c232-a47e-660b-9147-316e-f3fd-9203
3. Download the songs from your elLIVE digital locker and begin enjoying your new digital entertainment package today!